MORLEY LIBRARY
184 PHELPS STREET
PAINESVILLE, OHIO 44077
(440) 352-3383

AMERICAN
WAR LIBRARY

★ ★ ★ ★

★ The Korean War ★

WEAPONS OF WAR

by Michael V. Uschan

LUCENT
BOOKS®

THOMSON
★
GALE

San Diego • Detroit • New York • San Francisco • Cleveland • New Haven, Conn. • Waterville, Maine • London • Munich

LIBRARY OF CONGRESS CATALOGING-IN-PUBLICATION DATA

Uschan, Michael V., 1948–
    Weapons of war / by Michael V. Uschan.
        p. cm. — (American war library. the Korean war)
Includes bibliographical references and index.
        ISBN 1-59018-263-4 (hardback)
    1. Korean War, 1950–1953.   2. United Nations—Armed Forces—Korea.   3.
United States—Armed Forces—Korea.   I. Title.   II. Series.
        DS918.8.U83 2003
        951'904'24—dc21
                                                    2002156195

Printed in the United States of America

★ Contents ★

Foreword 5

Introduction: An Unexpected War 7

Chapter 1: UN Naval Power Dominates 12

Chapter 2: The Korean War: Combat at Close Quarters . . 26

Chapter 3: Tanks, Artillery, and Other Infantry
    Support Weapons 39

Chapter 4: Aerial Warfare in the Korean War 53

Chapter 5: The Age of Jet Fighter Warfare Begins 66

Chapter 6: Psychological Warfare: Words
    as Weapons 79

Conclusion: The Weapon the United States
    Dared Not Use 93

Notes 98

For Further Reading 103

Works Consulted 104

Index 107

Picture Credits 112

About the Author 112

A Nation Forged by War

T he United States, like many nations, was forged and defined by war. Despite Benjamin Franklin's opinion that "There never was a good war or a bad peace," the United States owes its very existence to the War of Independence, one to which Franklin wholeheartedly subscribed. The country forged by war in 1776 was tempered and made stronger by the Civil War in the 1860s.

The Texas Revolution, the Mexican-American War, and the Spanish-American War expanded the country's borders and gave it overseas possessions. These wars made the United States a world power, but this status came with a price, as the nation became a key but reluctant player in both World War I and World War II.

Each successive war further defined the country's role on the world stage. Following World War II, U.S. foreign policy redefined itself to focus on the role of defender, not only of the freedom of its own citizens, but also of the freedom of people everywhere. During the Cold War that followed World War II until the collapse of the Soviet Union, defending the world meant fighting communism. This goal, manifested in the Korean and Vietnam conflicts, proved elusive, and soured the American public on its achievability. As the United States emerged as the world's sole superpower, American foreign policy has been guided less by national interest and more by protecting international human rights. But as involvement in Somalia and Kosovo prove, this goal has been equally elusive.

As a result, the country's view of itself changed. Bolstered by victories in World Wars I and II, Americans first relished the role of protector. But, as war followed war in a seemingly endless procession, Americans began to doubt their leaders, their motives, and themselves. The Vietnam War especially caused people to question the validity of sending its young people to die in places where they were not particularly wanted and for people who did not seem especially grateful.

While the most obvious changes brought about by America's wars have been geopolitical in nature, many other aspects of society have been touched. War often does not bring about change directly, but acts instead like the catalyst in a chemical reaction, accelerating changes already in progress.

Some of these changes have been societal. The role of women in the United States had been slowly changing, but World War II put thousands into the workforce and into uniform. They might have gone back to being housewives after the war, but equality, once experienced, would not be forgotten.

Likewise, wars have accelerated technological change. The necessity for faster airplanes and a more destructive bomb led to the development of jet planes and nuclear energy. Artificial fibers developed for parachutes in the 1940s were used in the clothing of the 1950s.

Lucent Books' American War Library covers key wars in the development of the nation. Each war is covered in several volumes, to allow for more detail, context, and to provide volumes on often neglected subjects, such as the kamikazes of World War II, or weapons used in the Civil War. As with all Lucent Books, notes, annotated bibliographies, and appendixes such as glossaries give students a launching point for further research. In addition, sidebars and archival photographs enhance the text. Together, each volume in The American War Library will aid students in understanding how America's wars have shaped and changed its politics, economics, and society.

An Unexpected War

In the early hours of June 25, 1950, ninety thousand soldiers of the North Korean People's Army (NKPA) attacked South Korea. Advancing quickly and almost effortlessly behind powerful T-34 tanks, the Communist invaders sliced through the outnumbered, poorly equipped South Korean soldiers guarding the border the two countries shared.

The invasion was the first military confrontation of the Cold War, the battle for global domination that began after World War II between Communist countries led by the Soviet Union and democratic nations led by the United States. Following World War II, Korea had been divided in half, with North Korea falling under control of the Soviet Union and South Korea becoming an ally of the United States.

The surprise attack shocked the world in much the same way the Japanese aerial assault on Pearl Harbor, Hawaii, had on December 7, 1941. And just as Pearl Harbor sent the United States hurtling into World War II, the dawn attack pushed America into the Korean War. Even though the United States had not been directly attacked, its leaders believed the nation had to meet the Communist challenge in South Korea in order to preserve their way of life. "By God, I'm going to let them have it,"[1] was President Harry S. Truman's immediate and feisty response when he was told what had happened.

Despite Truman's militant resolve to help South Korea, the United States was singularly unprepared to save the country from Communist aggression. Even U.S. Army general Matthew B. Ridgway would admit years later that when the war began, "we were in a state of shameful unreadiness."[2]

Why America Was Unprepared

There were three main reasons why the United States was unprepared for the Korean War. First, because Truman and

The United Nations was swift in deploying troops to Korea after the Communist North Korean People's Army attacked South Korea in 1950.

other U.S. leaders had always believed that if the Cold War did erupt into violence it would happen in Europe, the United States had placed most of its military equipment and strength there. Thus, when North Korea attacked, America had few soldiers and little equipment available in Asia to defend South Korea, a nation it had never considered a major trouble spot.

Second, the American armed forces were weakened after World War II. America had emerged from that conflict as the world's most powerful nation both militarily and economically. But to reunite soldiers with their families, who were loudly demanding their return as soon as possible, and to concentrate on peacetime domestic issues, such as jobs and housing for returning veterans, the nation slashed its armed forces. Thus, the number of men and women in uniform had fallen from nearly 12 million in 1945 to about 2 million in 1950.

America had also failed since World War II to update and preserve its military equipment, which meant that many of the weapons, ships, planes, and support equipment military personnel needed to fight in Korea were in poor shape. U.S. soldiers arrived there only to discover that some weapons were not fit for combat—guns jammed, shells failed to explode, radios did not work, and trucks they needed for transport would not start. Although historian John Toland considers Truman's decision to aid Korea "courageous," he maintains it "could not have come at a worse time [because] the state of the U.S. military was deplorable."[3]

Not Ready for Conventional War

This critical lack of manpower and supplies can be traced directly to the third and most important reason the United States was unprepared for the Korean War—its success in forcing Japan to surrender in August 1945 by dropping atomic bombs on Hiroshima and Nagasaki. Following World War II, many military and political leaders believed the atomic bomb made their nation so strong that it would never have to fight another conventional war, one in which soldiers, sailors, and pilots battled each other for an extended period. In fact, in 1948 at Maxwell Field in Alabama, a U.S. Air Force seminar was convened on this theme: "Is there any further need for a ground force?"[4]

Instead, U.S. leaders believed that the threat of atomic destruction they wielded would scare other countries from challenging America. But the North Koreans called their bluff; they believed the United States would not unleash the horror of atomic bombs to protect a small, unimportant country so far from its shores, so they attacked anyway.

North Korea won this deadly political gamble for one main reason: Truman and other U.S. leaders feared that using the bomb could have ignited a far wider war, one that might have led to a nuclear reprisal against it by the Soviet Union, which had developed its own atomic bomb. As historian Joseph C. Goulden explains, "Korea shattered the American illusion that atomic weaponry had outmoded the foot soldier."[5]

A Conventional War

The United States thus found itself in the kind of war it thought it would never have to fight again, one that featured guns and tanks and bayonets instead of nuclear bombs. Although the Korean War featured several innovations in weaponry, including the first combat clashes between jet airplanes, most of the combat in this conflict was not much different from the fighting that had taken place during World War II and the other twentieth-century wars that came before it.

The reason combat in Korea was so reminiscent of the global conflict that had ended only five years earlier was that it was fought, almost exclusively, with the same weapons. The rifles, machine guns, hand grenades, tanks, mortars, ships, and many of the airplanes were the same ones that had been used in World War II, some of the weapons being surplus military matériel left over from that conflict.

Because it was an outgrowth of the Cold War, the participants were supplied by this global conflict's two main contenders. The Soviet Union manufactured most of the weapons that the North Korean and Chinese soldiers wielded. And although the effort to save South Korea was authorized by the United Nations (UN), the worldwide peacekeeping organization formed at the end of World War II, it was the United States that provided a majority of the manpower and war matériel for UN forces.

This surrogate role that the Cold War opponents played in arming participants created the conflict's supreme irony. During World War II, the Soviet Union and the United States had worked as allies to defeat Germany. Now, they were on opposite sides in the Korean War.

The Weapons That Made War Possible

In fact, one historian believes that if the Soviet Union had not been so generous in

UN forces in Korea used many of the same tanks and weaponry that helped the Allies to victory in World War II.

arming North Korea, there might not have been a war at all. George Forty, a British tank commander with UN forces in Korea, explains that the Soviet Union helped North Korea build an army that was twice as large (nearly two hundred thousand soldiers) and much better equipped than that of South Korea's military. Forty also claims that North Korea's superiority in weapons was the key factor that led to war: "Most importantly, they had the weapons for a successful . . . 'Blitzkrieg' [an overpowering and swift initial attack]—the best tanks of World War II, the T-34 which mounted a hard hitting 85 mm [millimeter] gun, and over 200 Yak fighters [planes]. Without these weapons there could have been no aggression."[6] The North Korean invaders used planes and tanks to help overwhelm their South Korean opponents, who had none of their own. They could only fight back weakly with rifles, carbines, and other small arms that could not withstand such firepower.

When the Americans entered the conflict, they would eventually bring in weapons that were as good as, if not better than, anything the Communist forces had. But throughout the war, as in the first few days when North Korea's military advantage was key to its successful invasion, the types of weapons each side had played an important role in how they could wage war, and in the outcome of the fighting.

UN Naval Power Dominates

An ancient Korean proverb warns, "A shrimp is crushed in the battle of the whales."[7] This simple adage is a fitting commentary for the Korean War, in which both South and North Korea were battered in a war that was actually an extension of the ongoing global battle between the Cold War superpowers, the Soviet Union and the United States. This military mismatch was most evident in the comparative naval strengths of the two sides, in which the United Nations (UN) was the "whale" and North Korea the "shrimp."

Neither North Korea nor China, the Communist ally that helped it wage the conflict, had a substantial navy. By contrast, the UN, mainly thanks to the U.S. Navy, had hundreds of ships, including giant aircraft carriers and battleships that dwarfed the few small Communist boats set against it as surely as the whale did the shrimp.

Even though UN forces had no rival navy to fight, Korea's geography made sea power an important factor in the conflict. North and South Korea are located on a peninsula, a long finger of land that dangles from the underbelly of China and is surrounded on three sides by water—on the east and south by the Sea of Japan and on the west by the Yellow Sea. And although the sea had always been important to the livelihood and culture of Koreans, naval historian George W. Baer notes that North Korea was singularly ill equipped to wage naval war: "There were only 45 vessels in the North Korean Navy. Most of them were torpedo boats or gunboats, and both types [of small craft] were easily destroyed or diverted by the Americans. China, which entered the war at the end of November 1950, posed no naval threat."[8]

Except for a few minor skirmishes between opposing ships in the opening days of the war, there were no sea battles. UN ships, however, still played a key role. In *The Korean War: No Victors, No Vanquished*, Stan-

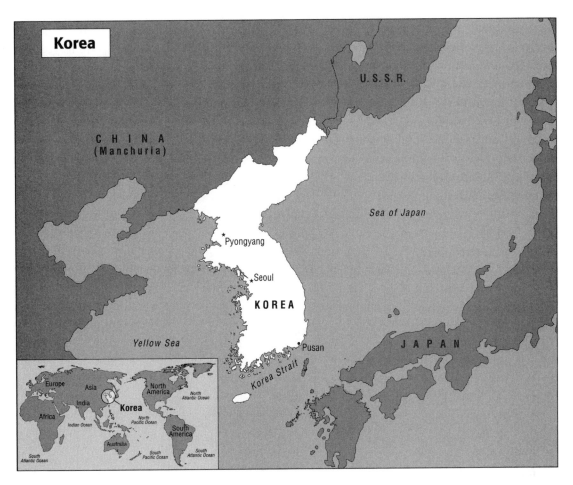

ley Sandler explains the importance of the UN's overwhelming edge in naval strength:

> Primarily, UN naval power made it possible to bring to the peninsula the troops and equipment needed to save the Republic of Korea. Second in importance, the UN navies were able to blockade North Korea far more tightly than could [its airplanes]. The Communist forces were *not* able to resupply their troops through [seaports such as] Wonsan or Hungham. Had they been able to do so, the UN position, at least in the first months of the war or in early 1951, could have been even more precarious.[9]

Early Setbacks

The stunning attack by North Korea that began the war on June 25, 1950, caught the United States by surprise. It also caught the powerful nation unprepared to respond to a military emergency half a world away.

The effects of America's military hibernation following World War II were evident during the opening weeks of the Korean War when Task Force Smith, the first small group of soldiers dispatched by President Harry S. Truman, arrived to help defend South Korea. There were too few soldiers, they had no heavy weapons that could stop North Korean tanks, and much of their equipment malfunctioned because it was too old or had not been stored properly.

Units of the U.S. Eighth Army were no match for the North Koreans, who outnumbered them and had superior weapons. The result was that American soldiers, who had believed they could easily defeat the North Korean invaders, wound up retreating until they were hemmed into a small area on South Korea's eastern coast. This angered officers like Lt. Col. Charles B. Smith, leader of Task Force Smith. As Smith later noted, there was nothing else he could do but fall back before the advancing North Koreans because he had not had enough men or the proper equipment to stop them: "To stand and die, or to try to get the remains of my Task Force out of there? I could last, at best, only another hour, and then lose everything I had. I chose to try to get out, in hopes that we would live to fight another day."[10]

The Navy to the Rescue

The situation was so bleak in the first few weeks of the war that UN officials feared

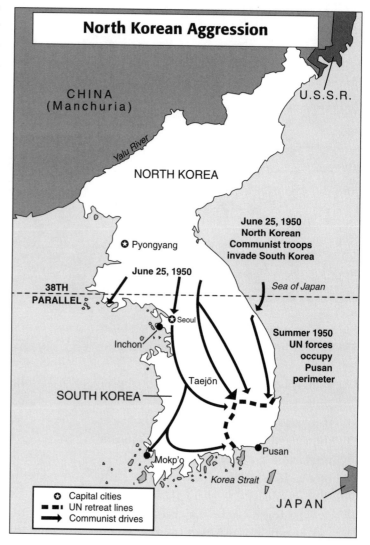

North Korean Aggression

CHINA
(Manchuria)

U.S.S.R.

Yalu River

NORTH KOREA

⊙ Pyongyang

June 25, 1950
North Korean
Communist troops
invade South Korea

June 25, 1950

38TH
PARALLEL

Sea of Japan

⊙ Seoul

Inchon

Summer 1950
UN forces
occupy
Pusan
perimeter

Taejŏn

SOUTH KOREA

● Pusan

Mokp'o

Korea Strait

JAPAN

⊙ Capital cities
UN retreat lines
Communist drives

the advancing Communists might force their soldiers to abandon Korea entirely. It was then that the U.S. Navy helped prevent a disaster by forming a floating link between Korea and Japan, where the United States had men and supplies in abundance. Navy historian Joseph H. Alexander explains,

The convoys [groups of ships] represented truly a lifeline to the Eighth Army in the early autumn of 1950, providing desperately needed reinforcements [soldiers] and heavier weapons. Ground forces especially required Pershing M-26 heavy tanks with 90 mm [millimeter] main guns to counter the Soviet-built T-34 tanks that had proved almost unstoppable thus far in the war.[11]

The men and war matériel that navy ships transported to Korea helped strengthen UN forces enough to make a stand at the South Korean city of Pusan and halt the Communist advance. In those first few weeks of the war, UN ships were also quickly and easily destroying the few small boats that composed the North Korean navy. And beginning on July 3, planes launched from two aircraft carriers—the USS *Valley Forge* and the British HMS *Triumph*—began attacking airfields in P'yongyang, North Korea's capital, and other targets that were beyond the cruising range of U.S. Air Force planes still based in Japan. The aerial assault

launched from these ships helped destroy most of North Korea's planes and weakened its ground forces.

Several decades later Adm. Sergei G. Gorshkov, who commanded the Soviet Union's navy during the 1970s, commented that without the UN's superior naval strength, early in the war its forces might not have survived. Claimed Gorshkov, "Without wide, active use of the fleet, the interventionists [United Nations] could hardly have escaped military defeat in Korea."[12]

The UN Fleet—Battleships and Aircraft Carriers

The majority of the hundreds of UN ships that fought in the Korean War was from the U.S. Navy. The biggest of these vessels included four battleships that had won acclaim during World War II—the *Iowa*, *Missouri*, *New Jersey*, and *Wisconsin*—and aircraft carriers such as the *Essex*, *Lexington*, *Princeton*, *Valley Forge*, and *Yorktown*. Although no more than three ever served in Korea at the same time, over thirty U.S. carriers fought there.

Battleships were the biggest military ships afloat. The *Missouri*, for example, was of titanic size. Nicknamed "the Mighty Mo," it was 887 feet long, almost 210 feet tall, slightly over 108 feet wide, weighed forty-five thousand tons empty, and carried a crew of over twenty-four hundred officers and enlisted men. It could reach speeds of thirty-two knots. One knot is a speed equal to one nautical mile an hour,

or 1.15 miles per hour; a nautical mile is 6,076 feet, slightly longer than a mile on land, which is 5,280 feet.

Battleships were designed to fight other ships, but they could also provide combat support. A battleship's heaviest armaments were nine sixteen-inch guns that could hurl shells twenty-three miles. Each of the rounds weighed between 1,700 and 2,700 pounds, and it took six 110-pound powder bags to fire them. The ship also had twelve five-inch guns that could shoot shells nine miles. Stationed in Norfolk, Virginia, when the war began,

The USS Missouri fires its sixteen-inch guns toward a North Korean target. U.S. Navy battleships played an important role during the early stages of the Korean War.

the *Missouri* was the first battleship to arrive in Korea on September 14, 1950. With no ships to fight, the *Missouri*'s big guns were used to strike coastal areas and inland targets.

Aircraft carriers were also huge. The *Valley Forge* was 888 feet long, over 147 feet high, 93 feet wide through its hull (body), and weighed 27,100 tons. The ship was topped by a flight deck—the long, flat area on which planes landed and took off—that was 862 feet long and 108 feet wide. The average aircraft carrier transported ninety planes. Navy plans included Skyraiders and Corsairs, which carried small loads of bombs, and Panthers, fighter planes that helped protect the other aircraft during aerial missions.

The *Valley Forge* was powered by steam turbines that generated 150,000 horsepower and could travel at thirty-three knots. Vast ships like this were complex to operate, requiring more than thirty-four hundred crew members, a population larger than many small American communities. The *Valley Forge* was armed with a dozen five-inch guns, over seventy machine guns, and antiaircraft guns.

The U.S. Navy had many other types of vessels that aided the war effort, including cruisers and destroyers. These slightly smaller ships provided offensive punch against other vessels, such as submarines, as well as against land targets. There were also scores of different specialty ships: oilers that carried fuel to run other ships; hospital vessels that tended the wounded; landing ships that transported men and equipment to shore during amphibious landings (in which soldiers were transferred from larger ships to land); minesweepers that destroyed

A Scary Landing on a Carrier

It was never easy landing a plane on an aircraft carrier, and sometimes it could be quite dangerous. In late 1952 navy pilot Jim Service served off the coast of Korea on the USS *Valley Forge*. In *No Bugles, No Drums: An Oral History of the Korean War*, edited by Rudy Tomedi, Service describes a harrowing landing in his F9F Panther fighter plane:

> A threat to your existence as a carrier pilot was a bad landing. I had a few of those. On one occasion I was coming in and I got my signal to land from the LSO [landing signals officer] standing out there on the deck with the two signal flags. But the signal flag was a little late. My instinct was to fly off and come around for another try, because taking a late cut, as we called it, meant you were going to land awfully far up the deck. But the signals you get from the LSO are absolutely mandatory. When he says cut [land] you better cut. Ever hear that old ex-

pression, flying on a wing and a prayer? That's the feeling I had coming in. I took the late signal, came in, touched down well forward, and although I succeeded in collapsing the nose gear on my airplane, it stayed on the deck. It was a heart-stopping moment for me.

Service had been worried he could have skidded off the deck into the water, which could be disastrous:

> You're not going to be in the water for long before you're completely incapacitated by the cold. If they didn't fish you out within minutes, it was goodbye. That was a greater fear, I think, than getting shot down. Going into the drink. We lost a couple of pilots that way. Neither one was in the water long, but they both froze to death before we could get them back aboard the ship.

enemy mines placed in the sea; repair ships; and submarines.

Many of the ships the UN depended on, including all the battleships except the *Missouri*, had been deactivated and placed in storage docks following World War II. They were now brought back into service and would play a vital part in changing the course of the Korean War.

MacArthur's Daring Plan

By August 1950 UN forces had stopped the North Korean advance at Pusan. They did this by establishing the Pusan Perimeter, a rectangular fortified defensive line about one hundred miles long and forty miles wide, which was so heavily fortified that the Communists could not break through it.

Despite the success of the Pusan Perimeter in stopping UN forces from being overrun, they remained in a vulnerable position. The North Koreans had captured much of South Korea, including Seoul, its capital, and still had UN and Republic of Korea (ROK) ground troops almost entirely surrounded. It was then that Gen. Douglas MacArthur, who had been placed in command of all UN forces, came up with a master stroke of strategy—one that depended on naval power to succeed.

On August 23 MacArthur met with other top military officials to propose a daring amphibious landing, a tactic he had utilized during World War II in many successful battles against Japanese forces.

The target would be Inchon, a port city on South Korea's west coast 110 miles behind enemy lines. MacArthur's bold idea was part of a wider strategy in which the infantry that the navy would put ashore would win back Seoul, which was twenty miles away, and then divide and weaken the NKPA.

However, Inchon was a difficult place to land. As Lt. Comdr. Arlie G. Capps remembers, "We drew up a list of every natural and geographical handicap [to such a mission]—and Inchon had 'em all."[13] To reach its harbor, UN ships had to advance along a narrow ten-mile waterway called Flying Fish Channel, which was shallow and at low tide had large mud flats that could trap ships. Another negative was that the entrance was guarded by Wolmi-do (Moon Tip) Island; from the hills that topped the island, North Korean guns could fire on UN ships.

The most glaring problem was that if just one ship was seriously damaged or became stranded on the mud flats, it could obstruct the channel and doom the landing. Despite the disadvantages presented to him, MacArthur still wanted to land at Inchon: "The very arguments . . . made as to the impracticalities involved will tend to ensure for *me* the element of surprise. For the North Korean commander will reason that no one would be so brash as to make such an attempt. I can almost hear the ticking of the second hand of destiny. We must act now or we will die. We shall land at Inchon, and *I* shall crush them."[14]

Gen. Douglas MacArthur's daring strategy to invade the port of Inchon was key to recapturing Seoul.

Operation Chromite

Planning immediately began for what was dubbed Operation Chromite. Despite reservations some naval officers still had, they threw themselves into assembling a fleet of 230 ships for the complex landing. They were undoubtedly spurred on by a remark that MacArthur made to Adm. Forrest Sherman: "The navy has never let me down in the past and it will not let me down this time."[15]

The ships that would capture Inchon were called Joint Task Force Seven, and were commanded by U.S. Navy vice admiral Arthur D. Struble. Although most were U.S.

ships, Great Britain, Canada, Australia, New Zealand, France, and the Republic of Korea contributed some vessels to the war fleet. U.S. and Japanese merchant cargo ships were also pressed into duty to transport the soldiers and supplies the landing required.

The infantry landing force totaled 71,339 men and was made up of units from the First Marine Division, Seventh Army Infantry Division, and two ROK regiments. In addition to large transport ships that brought the men to Inchon, the U.S. Navy had to assemble 120 small landing craft that would ferry soldiers and equipment to their attack points on land. The ships included four dozen vessels with the odd name of landing ship tank (LST). An LST was 328 feet long, 50 feet wide, could carry twenty-one hundred tons, and had doors in its forward bow that opened outward to a width of 14 feet. LSTs could transport most military vehicles, including as many as twenty tanks at one time.

It took several weeks to organize the landing force, partly because some ships needed to travel to Korea from other parts of the world. The ships and men were assembled in Kobe, Japan, the invasion plans carefully crafted, and a final date determined. The UN would invade Inchon on September 15, 1950.

LST: Vital to the Inchon Landing

The landing ship tank (LST) is a long, narrow ship that does not look very impressive. But in *Assault from the Sea*, a history of the Inchon landing written for the U.S. Navy by Curtis A. Utz, the author discusses the LST:

> The Landing Ship Tank (LST), which proved so crucial to UN success at Inchon, was developed during World War II to deploy tanks, vehicles and critical supplies directly onto assault beaches soon after infantry troops stormed ashore. The ships used a ballast system that allowed them to operate effectively on the open ocean, in shallow coastal waters and on the beach. The LST had a 328-foot length and 50-foot beam and could carry a 2,100-ton load. These ships were the stars of many World War II amphibious operations, and their crews proudly served in them; but because the LST could only must 10 knots of speed, sailors sometimes referred to them as "large, slow targets."

Utz notes that many of the four dozen LSTs that took part in the landing came from Japan, where they had been used for a wide variety of purposes by the Japanese in recovering from World War II. Lt. Erwin J. Hauber said the LST he received from Japan was filthy, had "rats bigger than footballs," and had the "penetrating odor of fish heads and urine." Utz describes how space on one such LST was converted into a medical facility:

> When Lieutenant Leslie H. Joslin was ordered to set up an operating room on board *LST 898* . . . Joslin's resourceful team scrubbed the small, filthy space assigned to them, brought on board a mountain of supplies, "scrounged" medicines from the Army and installed an operating table that they had removed from mothballed U.S. ships tied up . . . since World War II.

The Inchon Landing

Operation Chromite began on September 13 when UN naval forces began destroying enemy fortifications, coastal artillery batteries, and other targets in and around Inchon. The firepower to weaken Inchon's defenses before the landing came from planes that took off from aircraft carriers and destroyers and other ships that shelled enemy positions. After one bombing run, a pilot from the *Valley Forge* remarked on the damage he had seen from his plane: "The whole island looked like it had been shaved."[16]

The landing commenced just after midnight on September 15, when eighteen ships began making their way up Flying Fish Channel. At 5:08 A.M. they dropped anchor in the harbor and U.S. Marines began climbing over the sides of the bigger ships into smaller landing craft, which took them to shore. At 6:33 A.M., marines stormed the beaches of Wolmi-Do. Meeting little resistance, they secured the small island by 8:00 A.M., and only seventeen marines were wounded. The powerful preinvasion bombardments and the efficiency of the landing forces were such an overwhelming combination that many Communist defenders quickly surrendered.

But as the troops were securing the island the tide began receding, requiring

UN ships to pull back or be trapped in mud flats. It was not until 2:45 P.M., when the tide rose again, that the second round of landings could begin after yet another intense air and surface bombardment. Marines waded ashore at three beaches and climbed over seawalls that surrounded the city's industrial and port facilities. They were again met with only light resistance from the estimated 2,000 North Korean soldiers defending Inchon. Only 20 U.S. Marines were killed and 179 were wounded during the entire landing, which was a smashing success thanks to skillful planning and execution. MacArthur showered praise on the naval power that had accomplished the difficult mission: "The Navy and Marines have never shone more brightly than this morning."[17]

The military force that landed made its way to Seoul, recapturing it on September 26. The resurgent UN troops also successfully attacked the North Korean army, sending it reeling backward and taking more than 125,000 soldiers prisoner. It was the navy-powered landing that helped turn the tide of war in favor of the UN, which, in the next two months, reclaimed all of South Korea and advanced deep into North Korea.

Four UN landing ship tanks unload military equipment and men on a Korean beach during the Inchon invasion.

The Sitting Ducks of Inchon

One of the bravest missions prior to the landing at Inchon was conducted on September 13 by six destroyers that became known as "the Sitting Ducks." At 10:10 A.M. that day the *Mansfield, De Haven, Lyman K. Swenson, Collett, Gurke*, and *Henderson* sailed up Flying Fish Channel and pulled up before Wolmi-do Island. Their mission was to be living targets for the island's gun emplacements so that they could be spotted and targeted for destruction. Several ships were damaged and one sailor was killed—Lt. David H. Swenson, who was the nephew of his ship's namesake. Harvey Headland, who served on the *Mansfield*, describes the mission in the article "Sitting Ducks: Leading the Inchon Invasion" on a U.S. Navy website:

> As part of the plan to locate enemy gun positions on Wolmi-do, the destroyers would be sent in first, to tempt the gunners on the island to disclose their positions. The destroyers were required to enter the harbor at flood tide, anchor at the short stay, and be ready for anything. Thus they acquired the name they have held ever since: "The Sitting Ducks." . . . *Collett* and *Gurke* were the nearest to the fortified Wolmi-do, only some 700 yards away. [Firing] of the destroyers' 5-inch guns commenced. At first the shore batteries did not respond—but only for a few minutes. Then the shore batteries concentrated their fire on the ships closest: *Collett, Gurke*, and *Swenson. Collet* was hit five times, with five men wounded and her firing computer damaged. She moved out of range. *Gurke* was hit three times and sustained two men injured. *Swenson* was not hit, but Lieutenant Junior Grade David H. Swenson fell from a shell or fragment. Thus the "Sitting Ducks" accomplished their mission of causing the enemy to disclose their position and power. All this required less than an hour. [The *Mansfield*] exited the inner harbor, last in the column, without any damage to ship or personnel. I have been thankful to God ever since.

Mines at Wonsan

MacArthur wanted to use a similar amphibious landing to capture Wonsan. Located on the east coast, Wonsan was the finest port in Korea as well as a hub for rail and highway traffic; its capture would help UN forces to land and then transport soldiers and supplies needed for battle. But in October, when UN ships began moving in to plan the landing, they ran into the only North Korean naval weapon that was effective against them during the entire war—mines.

The port at Wonsan was littered with between two and four thousand sea mines.

There were two kinds of sea mines: contact mines, which floated on the surface, and magnetic mines, which lay on the ocean floor but could rise to clamp onto metal hulls. On October 12 two minesweepers—the USS *Pirate* and USS *Pledge*—were sunk within the space of eleven minutes while trying to clear mines; several other ships were also damaged. The mine threat delayed the plan to capture Wonsan by eight days and killed or wounded over two hundred sailors, leading Rear Adm. Allan E. Smith to scornfully remark, "We have lost control of the seas to a nation without a navy, using pre–World War I weapons, laid by vessels [sampans, which were wooden fishing boats] that were utilized at the time of the birth of Christ."[18]

The effort to clear the mines took so long that by the time it was safe enough for an amphibious landing on October 25, UN soldiers had already arrived by land to capture Wonsan. It was one of the most embarrassing moments of the war for the U.S. Navy. During the war, sea mines proved to be the only effective naval weapon the Communists had; all five of the UN ships that were sunk went down after hitting mines, and most of the eighty-seven ships damaged in action were struck by mines.

The Hungnam Evacuation

UN successes in the fall of 1950 in recapturing all of South Korea and much of North Korea, however, were reversed with lightning rapidity in November when a half-million Chinese soldiers entered the war and quickly overwhelmed UN ground forces. Before the UN army could stop the advancing Communists, they had taken back all of North Korea, including Inchon.

The U.S. Navy now had to work in reverse in Inchon and Wonsan by evacuating UN personnel and equipment. The most dramatic rescue effort took place in December at Hungnam. Historian George W. Baer, who claims it was "another amphibious success" for the U.S. Navy, describes the giant effort that involved many vessels, including a battleship, four aircraft carriers, and twenty-two destroy-ers: "Navy ships laid a wall of gunfire in front of an Army-held barrier and, behind the barrier, took off the troops. [In the evacuation] 193 ships removed 196,000 people, 350,000 tons of cargo, and 17,500 vehicles."[19] The evacuees included more than 90,000 Korean civilians fleeing the Communists. Sailors aboard the *Missouri* remembered seeing LSTs, which normally carried soldiers and tanks, loaded with unusual items: "Korean children, goats, chickens—the damnedest collection of things you ever saw."[20] When the port city was evacuated, navy underwater demolition teams blew up the equipment, supplies, and weapons that remained so the Communists would not get them.

Blockading Ports

For the rest of the Korean War, U.S. Navy control of the sea lanes continued to be vital because it allowed UN ships to freely deliver supplies and men to battle. UN aircraft carriers also launched waves of attack planes to hit strategic targets while battleships and other vessels provided offensive firepower for land battles. UN naval forces also continued to be the war's transportation giant: Six out of every seven men who fought in Korea arrived by ship; for every ton of freight that was delivered by airplane, 270 tons came by ship.

One of the navy's most important missions in the final two years of the war was to blockade North Korean ports to prevent Communists from receiving supplies.

The major enemy port was Wonsan, which Communists had recaptured during the Chinese offensive in late 1950. UN naval forces, however, rendered Wonsan inoperable for the rest of the war through prolonged attacks. From February 16, 1951, until the day the fighting stopped, ships shelled and bombarded Wonsan for 861 straight days, the longest siege in modern U.S. naval history. On March 29, 1951, after Wonsan had been hit for forty-one straight days, Rear Adm. Allan F. Smith commented, "In Wonsan you cannot walk in the streets, you cannot sleep anywhere in the twenty-four hours, unless it is the sleep of death."[21] By war's end, Wonsan had been reduced to a mass of ruins, with hardly a single building still standing.

Sampan Versus Destroyer

The overwhelming naval superiority that allowed UN forces to shut down ports like Wonsan and contributed to UN success in other areas of the Korean War is symbol-

A squadron of American F4U Corsairs cruises above the USS Boxer *before a strike. Aircraft carriers launched countless waves of fighter planes during the war.*

Deadly Mines

During the Korean War, sea mines were the only real weapon the North Koreans or Chinese were able to deploy against UN ships. In *Fleet Operations in a Mobile War*, U.S. Navy historian Joseph H. Alexander explains that on October 1, 1950, when mines hit the minesweeper *Magpie*, it was the first U.S. naval vessel sunk in enemy action since World War II; the captain of the *Magpie* and twenty crewmen died. Chief Boatswain's Mate Vail P. Carpenter, one of a dozen wounded survivors, explains what it was like when the mine went off: "There was a tremendous explosion and the entire forward portion of the ship, forward of the stack [engine smokestack], appeared to explode. The remainder of the ship immediately started to set-

tle [into the water] by the head [the front of the boat]."

An even worse day came October 12 when two minesweepers—the *Pirate* and the *Pledge*—both sank at Wonsan. The two ships combined suffered thirteen deaths and eighty-nine injuries. Alexander quotes Lt. Richard O. Young, who was commanding the *Pledge* when it went down: "The starboard side of the hull, just forward of the superstructure, was rent [broken open] from below the waterline to the topside. The deck, at this location, was also sheared from gunwale [side of the boat] to gunwale. The silence that reigned throughout the ship indicated that casualties were very heavy. I therefore gave the order to abandon ship."

ized by an incident in November 1951 witnessed by Vincent Walsh, a machinist mate aboard the USS *Beatty*. Walsh recalls that a lone North Korean in a sampan—a small wooden fishing boat—was placing a mine in the water when he was sighted by a destroyer, a ship that weighs over two thousand tons and was 376 feet long. Walsh explains what happened: "This guy started rowing for all he was worth, trying

to get back to shore, and we started firing our main batteries at him. It was like a giant playing with a little toy. There was this rock he tried to hide behind, but it disintegrated under one of our shells, and he did too."[22]

UN ships were as dominant over the few vessels the Communists had as that destroyer was over the small wooden-hulled fishing boat. It was strictly no contest.

Chapter 2

The Korean War: Combat at Close Quarters

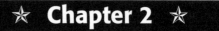

For the most part, the Cold War's first armed conflict was almost old-fashioned in the weapons soldiers on both sides carried to battle and how they wielded them. James Brady, who fought as a U.S. Marine lieutenant, describes ground combat in his memoir, *The Coldest War*:

> In some ways, it wasn't a modern war at all, more like Flanders or the Somme [World War I] or even the Wilderness campaign [the Civil War]. There were jets and tanks and warships but you didn't see them very often. Korea was fought mostly by infantrymen with M-1 rifles and machine guns and hand grenades and mortars. Men who fought in France in 1917 [during World War I] would have understood Korea; [Confederate general Robert E.] Lee's and [Union general Ulysses S.] Grant's men would have recognized it.[23]

An earthbound infantry soldier, Brady's comments tend to ignore the contributions made by the military's air and sea branches. However, Brady's infantry bias does nothing to detract from his main point: Although the weapons soldiers carried had improved—the M1, for example, was more accurate and could kill at far greater distances than the Civil War musket—the basic way that infantry soldiers fought—at close quarters, sometimes face to face—had not drastically changed from past wars.

The ground-level experience of the Korean War was an intensely personal confrontation between opposing soldiers, one that was brutal, dehumanizing, chaotic, and frightening in a way rarely experienced by pilots and sailors who were physically removed from such carnage. In fact, the combat Brady describes fits a far earlier definition of war. Carl von Clausewitz, a nineteenth-century German general considered one of history's greatest military tacticians, once wrote, "Close combat, man to man, is plainly to be regarded as the real basis of combat."[24]

For hundreds of thousands of soldiers, this was the kind of fighting they experienced. The weapons they wielded determined how they fought in those clashes as well as who won or lost, lived or died.

Basic UN Weapons

The basic handheld U.S. infantry weapon was the M1, a rifle also carried by Republic of Korea forces and infantry soldiers from other countries who fought under the United Nations banner. Although a few larger nations, such as England, equipped their troops with their own military arms, the United States supplied M1s and other weapons to foreign soldiers who helped it wage this conflict.

The M1 was a semiautomatic weapon, which meant a soldier could fire one shot or several rapidly in succession by continually pulling the trigger; it had an internal metal case, called a clip or magazine,

A regimental combat team positions itself for a ground attack. Man-to-man fighting was an important battle tactic in Korea.

British Arms Fought as Well

Although most U.S. allies in the Korean War fought with American weapons, soldiers sent by Great Britain brought their own arms. Most of the weapons were similar to their U.S. counterparts, and they used them in the same way tactically. The biggest exception was the rifles they carried—the British rifle was a bolt-action weapon that fired slower than the semiautomatic American M1. From April 22 through 25, 1951, members of the Gloucester Regiment fought for their lives at the Imjim River while surrounded by Chinese soldiers. The following account of part of that battle, from *The Korean War: History and Tactics* by David Rees, shows the kind of British weapons involved in the fighting:

> Armed with the bolt-action Lee Enfield rifle which, in various forms, had given good service in both World Wars, each rifleman

instinctively went through the drill imposed by his musketry instruction: "Stay in the aim and count off your rounds . . . eight . . . nine . . . ten . . . insert fresh clip . . . one . . . two . . . three. . . ." The terrible rapid fire was thudding into [Chinese] battalions and decimating them, just as it had done with [German] assault columns at Mons [France] in 1914. In addition, the Bren light machine guns were hammering away in three- and four-round bursts, and the belt-fed Vickers [heavier machine guns] were scything through the enemy's ranks. Yet still the Chinese came on . . . each attack ending in a flurry of exchanged grenades and the rattle of sub-machine guns and pistols. Even as it sank into the ground another attack would be on the way in; in Korea the expression "Trigger Fatigue" had a very real meaning.

British servicemen board a ship in Southampton, Great Britain, headed to UN positions in Korea.

containing eight .30-caliber bullets. The caliber of a bullet refers to its diameter. By swiftly inserting new clips, a soldier could fire as many as thirty rounds per minute from a rifle that could hit targets accurately at distances over four hundred yards. The M1 weighed nine and a half pounds—one pound more when its bayonet, a long steel blade that extended from the barrel, was attached. Enlisted men carried the M1.

Although this rifle had changed little since being introduced in 1936 as the standard army weapon, soldiers still loved it. In a report prepared for the Eighth Army on weapon usage in the Korean War, S.L.A. Marshall wrote, "The issue rifle (M1) has performed adequately in Korea and is regarded by troops with a liking amounting to affection."[25]

The M1 could become a sniper rifle if some of its parts were reworked to make it shoot more accurately and if it had a scope, a device like a telescope that helps shooters aim at distant targets. There were even infrared scopes that allowed snipers to see targets at night. Snipers had used precision rifles to kill at long range in many wars, but this form of combat was not popular in Korea.

Officers and some other soldiers, such as company clerks in headquarters areas, carried the .30-caliber semiautomatic carbine, a shorter, lighter rifle only half the M1's weight. The carbine had a smaller, less powerful cartridge that reduced its range. To increase its firepower, the carbine had detachable box magazines that held fifteen or thirty rounds, the latter named the banana magazine because of its curved shape.

Although soldiers could hit targets at three hundred yards, many complained that the carbine was not powerful enough to seriously wound someone beyond fifty yards. Another reason the carbine was not popular was that its automatic mechanism tended to malfunction in the bitter cold of Korean winters.

Officers and soldiers who fought in tanks, manned artillery guns, or had other jobs that made it difficult to carry rifles or carbines, were issued pistols. The standard U.S. Army sidearm was the .45, a large, powerful semiautomatic pistol developed prior to World War I that was renowned for its ability to kill with one bullet. Although only accurate to about fifty yards, pistols were effective weapons in close-quarters combat.

Automatic Weapons

Although there were far fewer of them, infantry soldiers also fought with heavier, more powerful, but still portable fully automatic weapons capable of firing hundreds of rounds in a short period. This type of gun fires a continuous stream of bullets when its trigger is depressed.

The main automatic weapon was the Browning automatic rifle (BAR), which weighed 18.5 pounds and had a twenty-round box magazine that could be changed in a few seconds when emptied. Although the BAR could fire short bursts of a few bullets, it had a maximum rate of 550 bullets per minute. Each army platoon (a basic combat unit consisting of four nine-man squads) had two two-man BAR teams, and Marine Corps platoons had three such teams. The gunner fired the weapon, and the assistant gunner carried ammunition and helped load the BAR during fights.

The BAR was normally operated from a tripod, but if a soldier was strong enough he could pick it up and fire it. The BAR fired the same .30-caliber bullet as the M1 and was accurate up to six hundred yards. It could also fire more powerful rounds that could pierce armor—metal that protected tanks and other vehicles—or incendiary bullets that could puncture light armor and then ignite a fire inside the target with explosive chemicals contained in the round. In addition to the BAR, platoons also had .30-caliber light machine guns that fired more than five hundred rounds a minute; they were bigger and harder to transport than the BAR.

Grenades

In addition to guns, infantry soldiers used several types of hand grenades. The most common was the fragmentation grenade, a small pear-shaped object made of metal that would break into lethal bits when the explosive charge it contained detonated. The fragments had a killing radius of five to ten yards and could wound enemy soldiers fifty yards away.

After pulling a safety pin to arm it, a soldier threw the grenade like a baseball—normally less than thirty-five yards. When the grenade left the soldier's hand, a lever that he had depressed while holding it ignited a time-delay fuse that would explode the grenade in four to five seconds. This meant the soldier had to duck down quickly to avoid being injured. Soldiers tossed smoke grenades to hide troop movements from the enemy and white phosphorous grenades, which burned brilliantly for almost a minute, to illuminate the enemy at night.

Marshall notes that soldiers made the hand grenade a mainstay of battle, using it in nearly every fight: "Practically without exception, all in-fighting in Korea is attended by hand-grenade action. In comparison to the numbers engaged, use of the hand grenade by American troops in Korea is [higher than] in either World War I or II."[26]

Basic Communist Weapons

The weapons Communist forces fought with varied in many ways from those which UN forces carried. In *The Korean War: History and Tactics*, David Rees writes that "the difference in weapon types between the two armies is significant."[27] One main contrast was the wide variety of personal weapons North Korean and Chinese soldiers used in comparison to UN forces, whose arms were more standardized.

North Koreans generally fought with weapons manufactured by the Soviet Union. But the Chinese, in addition to

The Browning automatic rifle (left), or BAR, was lightweight enough to carry by hand and allowed infantry soldiers to fire more than five hundred bullets per minute.

basic Soviet weapons, also carried arms captured from the Japanese during World War II—from rifles to artillery pieces—as well as U.S. weapons seized from defeated Nationalist forces during China's civil war. During the Korean War, Communist soldiers also captured and used huge quantities of UN weapons.

The biggest difference between UN and Chinese infantry was that most Chinese soldiers did not carry rifles. Although Chinese soldiers had some Russian 7.62 millimeter (mm) carbines and 7.7 mm Japanese army rifles, they generally carried submachine guns. These weapons fired smaller, less powerful 7.62 mm pistol cartridges. Submachine guns were inaccurate except at close range and had less killing power than rifles; their only plus was a much more rapid rate of fire. The reasoning was that because most Communist soldiers were inaccurate shooters, they would be more dangerous with this weapon than with a rifle, even though those arms could kill at greater distances.

The standard was the Soviet Shpagin Pistolet-PulemyotShpagina (PPSh) 41 submachine gun, which U.S. soldiers dubbed the "burp gun" because of its staccato, rasping noise. The PPSh 41 held seventy-two rounds in a replaceable magazine and could fire one hundred rounds per minute if a soldier inserted a second magazine fast enough. It could fire short bursts or continuously until it ran out of bullets.

Soldiers also used the Tokarev semiautomatic 7.62 mm, the Soviet version of the BAR. Officers and some soldiers carried the Soviet Tokarev TT33, an eight-round, 7.62 mm semiautomatic pistol, and the Chinese 51, a copy of the TT33.

Two U.S. infantrymen keep enemy soldiers at bay with machine gun fire as a third tosses a fragmentation grenade into their post.

The Communists also used hand grenades extensively in battle, but their version of this basic weapon differed from those carried by UN forces. The Communist grenade had a conical explosive device mounted on a stick, making it easy to throw. Americans nicknamed it a "potato masher" because it looked like something a cook used to beat potatoes. The stick-type grenade was armed by unscrewing the wooden cap on top, which was connected by a string to the fuse; soldiers ignited the fuse by pulling the top off, and then they had several seconds to throw it. There were several versions of stick-type grenades, including a fragmentation one. They were less powerful than U.S. grenades and often only injured soldiers slightly; American soldiers generally held them in contempt as inferior weapons.

The Chinese also had many types of Soviet machine guns; they were similar in firepower to American guns and used a 7.62 mm cartridge. As with all Soviet-made weapons, they were reliable. In *This Kind of War*, author T.R. Fehrenbach states, "Russian weaponry has one marked characteristic; it is extremely rugged, of the simplest design consistent with efficiency, and very easy to maintain, making it in many cases more suitable of the equipping of peasant armies than the more sophisticated U.S. arms."[28]

Weapons Influence Tactics

The types of heavy weapons and support equipment the two sides had affected the way they fought. Although the personal weapons that Communists carried were adequate, they did not have as many artillery pieces, tanks and other armored vehicles, and trucks to transport soldiers and supplies as UN forces. Although this was generally a huge disadvantage, the lack of motorized vehicles gave Communists one big advantage—they could travel more quickly because they were not limited to roads like UN forces.

In *At War in Korea*, George Forty explains that early in the war "the more lightly equipped Chinese troops were ideally situated to the rugged Korean terrain and quickly nullified the superior firepower of their road-bound [opponents]."[29] The advantage Communists had in speedy movement helped them surround UN forces during combat, beat them to strategic positions, and achieve other military advantages over a slower-moving foe.

However, because UN planes controlled the skies, the Communists had to move and fight at night so that bomber and fighter planes would not decimate their ranks with bombs and bullets. The fact that Chinese troops almost always attacked at night helped make the battles strange and frightening, as did the way the Communists assaulted UN positions.

The Chinese charged in waves of massed humanity to the accompaniment of blaring bugles, horns, and whistles, which constituted their primitive signaling system. The scene was also lit up by flares, which were shot high into the sky and cast an eerie light on the frenzied assaults.

The massed attacks were all the more unnerving because so many Chinese soldiers charged all at once and because they did not seem to care if they lived or died. However, the "burp gun" they carried, ineffective except at close range, gave Communist soldiers no choice but to attack that way. Pvt. Fred Lawson, a Marine Corps rifleman, describes a mass charge in December 1950 while his unit was defending Toktong Pass near Hagaru; in the fierce fighting, only thirty-seven out of two hundred soldiers in Lawson's unit survived. Explains Lawson,

> They looked like a bunch of sheep swarming up the hill. None of us had ever seen anything like it. They didn't seem to have any training at all. They just came straight at us, like a mob, you couldn't help but hit them. And we were really stacking them up. But there were so many and they just kept coming. Pretty soon we were in it hand to hand. Gun butts, knives, fists. After I ran out of ammo I conked a couple with a helmet, swinging it by the strap.[30]

The tactics worked not only because there were so many Communist soldiers

Chinese Battle Tactics

In *At War in Korea*, military historian George Forty explains that the military strategy employed by the Chinese was the same that Communists led by Mao Tse-tung had formulated and then used to win control of China during that nation's civil war. The tactics Mao adopted were based on necessity—his army was not as well supplied as the Nationalist forces led by Chiang Kai-shek, who received hundreds of millions of dollars in arms and aid from the United States. When Chinese troops entered the Korean War, they had to fight under similar conditions, as Forty explains.

> Although the Chinese Reds were [mostly] a peasant army, it was also a first-rate army when judged by its own tactical and strategic standards. Military poverty [a lack of heavy weapons and other supplies] might be blamed for some of its deficiencies in arms and equipment, but its semi-guerrilla tactics were based on a mobility which could not be burdened with heavy weapons and transport. The Chinese coolie [common laborer] in the padded cotton uniform could do one thing better than any other soldier on earth: he could infiltrate around an enemy position in the darkness with unbelievable stealth. Only Americans who have had such an experience can realize what a shock it is to be surprised at midnight with the grenades and submachine gun slugs of gnomelike attackers who seem to rise out of the very earth. . . . A generation of warfare [in China] against material odds had established a pattern of attack which proved effective against armies possessing an advantage in arms and equipment.

assailing the UN forces but also because their military leaders were skillful strategists. Communist officers used their superior speed of movement to create clever ambushes, envelopments, and roadblocks that destroyed South Korean regiments and forced the battered Americans to retreat south across the Chongchon River.

UN tactics were almost exactly opposite those of the Chinese. The big difference was that UN soldiers usually attacked during daylight hours so they could be supported by planes, artillery pieces, and other heavy weapons. Another big advantage UN forces had in combat was that they could almost always count on receiving a steady stream of ammunition, food, and other vital supplies. The Communists had trouble reequipping their soldiers in the field, and during prolonged battles they often ran out of ammunition and food.

Static War

The Communists' superior mobility helped them in the fast-paced fighting that characterized the first year of the war, when the two sides kept battling up and down the length of the two war-torn nations. However, by the summer of 1951 the style of war had changed drastically. The two sides had now established a defensive line that angled in the east from forty miles north of the 38th parallel—the geographic border between the two countries before the war began—to a few miles below that line in the west.

This static war was the result of peace talks the two sides had begun to end the fighting. The first negotiating session began July 10, 1951, in Kaesong, and the talks continued until a cease-fire ended the fighting on July 27, 1953. During the two years that negotiations dragged on, the two sides waged a limited war, one in which they dug in along what became known as the main line of resistance (MLR) or demilitarized zone (DMZ), and they engaged in mostly small, though still deadly, attacks on each other. It was a static style of warfare, one that historian Rudy Tomedi explains was reminiscent of World War I: "During the last two years of the conflict the combatants fought almost exclusively from opposing trench lines, giving some of those who were familiar with the images of the 1914–18 trench warfare an eerie sense of deja vu."[31]

Deadly Combat

This last phase of the Korean War featured some of its most brutal close combat. It was in this type of war that opposing soldiers had to rely more than ever on rifles, grenades, and other weapons to stay alive.

The two sides were entrenched in deep tunnels, fortified bunkers, and caves in a deadly necklace that stretched 155 miles across the width of the two Koreas. In some places the distance between enemies was only hundreds of yards, but in other areas the deadly divide, called no-man's-land, was several miles deep. Military historian David Rees states, "This static war gave rise to the numerous little bloody battles for position which formed the only major actions of the stalemated war."[32]

The fights were often for control of hilltops that had generically assigned numbers but which the soldiers who fought for them gave dramatic, sometimes whimsical-sounding, names. There was Old Baldy, the Hook, and Pork Chop Hill, a height that was officially designated Hill 255 on military maps because that was its elevation in yards. Combat washed over this hill near the Yokkokchon River again and again from April to July. Charles Brooks, an infantry soldier, describes what it was like to defend the hill from a bunker strengthened by sandbags, rocks, and heavy timbers: "They [bunkers] had apertures in them where we could fire our weapons, and all we could do was fire everything we had and try to keep the Chinese away. It was like a movie where you see the soldiers popping away at the Indians from inside a fort, except that you're only too aware that it isn't a movie. But not scared. You're too busy to be scared."[33]

In addition to such full-scale assaults, there were smaller actions almost nightly when patrols from both sides set out to scout and fight in the desolate area between enemy lines. James Brady led many such missions. He explains that the combat that occurred was deadly, confusing,

Weapons Go Silent

The sound of combat is a loud, frightening mixture of all the weapons that are being used by both sides. First Lt. Robert J. Gerard of the 224th Infantry Regiment knew those sounds well. But the sweetest sound of all was when the weapons all began to go silent the night of July 27, 1953, when the cease-fire that ended the war went into effect. Gerard's account is from *Witness to War: Korea* by Rod Paschall:

> As twilight approached, there was a sense of excitement in the air. We had received strict instructions that all weapons firing was to cease promptly by 10 P.M. At about 8 P.M., as it grew dark, the occasional exchange of fire picked up in tempo. Rifle fire was reinforced with the chattering of automatic weapons. The mortars were reinforced with artillery which swooshed overhead on its way to some unseen enemy.

The Quad 50s [four .50-caliber machine guns mounted on a vehicle] assigned to support us laced the North Korean positions with a stream of fire. Both sides had picked up the pace and by 9:30 P.M., the exchange was at a peak. The air was thick with the acrid smell of gunpowder, mixed with clouds of dirt and dust; the sky was illuminated with one flare after another. At about 9:45 P.M. the firing began to fall off in reverse sequence. First, the artillery slowed, then the mortars, then the small arms. At 9:55 P.M. firing was limited to an occasional short burst from an automatic weapon. After a few more single rifle shots, it became deadly quiet. There was a sense of calm, a sense of relief. In the dark, you couldn't see it, but you could feel it.

UN officers smile as they read of a possible end to the fighting in Korea.

and primitive: "Sometimes, out there, two patrols would meet, hundreds of yards from their own lines. Then confusion became chaos, and they [combatants] killed the enemy and they killed each other. Who knew whom you were shooting in the night? The grenade, the knife, the shotgun, even the shovel and the ax were the weapons of the night patrols. It was a throwback, this war."[34]

Bayonets

Perhaps the most primitive weapon soldiers had was the bayonet, an ancient implement of war that had been used for centuries. At times during the Korean War, it became the most deadly weapon soldiers had. The bayonet was used in many battles—sometimes by design but more often out of necessity by a soldier whose rifle misfired or ran out of bullets.

The Korean War's most famous bayonet charge occurred February 7, 1951, in a heroic effort to capture Hill 180. Capt. Lewis L. Millett earned a Medal of Honor, the army's highest award for bravery, for leading that bayonet attack. Millett, who ordered the charge because he felt it was the only way to capture the position, explains how he used his bayonet to kill three soldiers:

I bayoneted [the first soldier he saw]. I guess the other two didn't realize I was that close. The next man reached for something but I bayoneted him—got him in the throat. At about that time the third man turned and—I was straddling a very narrow trench—he froze. He had a submachine gun but I guess the sight of me, red-faced and screaming, made him freeze. Otherwise he would have killed me. I lunged forward and the bayonet went into his forehead.[35]

Millett and his men killed eighteen enemy soldiers with their bayonets. That bayonet charge is considered the most well-executed and bravest since Cold Harbor, an 1864 Civil War battle in which Union soldiers unsuccessfully assaulted entrenched Confederates.

This most primitive of weapons was also used in January 1951 by members of the Fifth Cavalry in another fight for a hill, this one numbered 312. An official account of the attack shows how desperate the hand-to-hand struggle was between soldiers of the Fifth Cavalry's First Battalion and the heavily entrenched Communists:

The enemy delivered small arms fire and hurled grenades down on the advancing troopers, who hurled the grenades aside or attempted to throw them back. [When U.S. soldiers reached the top of the hill, Communists emerged from holes they had dug] to fight with rifles, and bayonets and spades. For a time, the battle hung in the balance; then the 3rd Platoon of A Company came charging up the hill with fixed bayonets. The enemy positions were

American soldiers fighting from inside a trench ready their artillery for an impending assault.

overwhelmed, although small hand-to-hand engagements took place for some time.[36]

A New Use for a Grenade

The weapons soldiers on both sides had were good ones, usually fulfilling the purpose for which they were made with deadly effectiveness. But, sometimes, if they were to survive, soldiers had to invent new ways to use their weapons.

In July 1950 army private Frank Baldwin Myers ran out of ammunition in a battle near Hadong. Armed only with a bayonet and a grenade, Myers was trying to sneak up on an enemy machine gun when he noticed a pair of shoes sticking out from some brush. It was then, writes

historian John Toland, that Myers found a new way to use his grenade: "A North Korean emerged swinging a long-barreled rifle at Myers. He felt helpless. He was standing with only a grenade in his hand. If he pulled the pin, he himself would probably be killed. He threw the grenade as if it were a rock. It struck the [enemy] in the stomach."[37] The blow to the North Korean's stomach stunned him just enough for Myers to grab the soldier's rifle and use it to kill him. It was one of many ways in which soldiers had to improvise to stay alive in the most brutal of all kinds of warfare—close combat.

Chapter 3

Tanks, Artillery, and Other Infantry Support Weapons

Infantry soldiers on both sides of the Korean War basically fought each other with weapons they carried—rifles, hand grenades, and bayonets. But whether ground troops were attacking the enemy or defending their own position, they were often supported in battle by other soldiers operating much more powerful weapons.

These bigger, more complex weapons included tanks, artillery, heavy machine guns, and flamethrowers. The soldiers who operated them required special training and were usually organized into separate military units. Their mission was not only to work with the infantry to defeat the enemy but also to help protect their fellow soldiers when they were endangered.

During the conflict United Nations forces, as they did in aerial and naval strength, enjoyed a vast superiority in such weapons. The wide array of such weapons that UN soldiers had at their disposal gave them yet another military advantage over their foes. As author George Forty states in *At War in Korea*. "At best the [Communist] infantry received little help from supporting arms."[38]

In the first few weeks of the war, however, the North Korean People's Army enjoyed a huge advantage in one of the key support weapons available: tanks.

Soviet Tanks

When the NKPA invaded South Korea on June 25, 1950, one main reason it overpowered Republic of Korea troops so easily was that the invaders had a weapon South Koreans could not stop—the Soviet-built T-34 tank. ROK troops had nothing strong enough to withstand the thirty-five-ton tanks, which blasted away at them with 85 mm cannons that shredded defenders and sent survivors fleeing for their lives.

The power of the tanks was immediately evident to Task Force Smith, the first U.S. Army contingent to help defend South

North Korean Tanks Are Unstoppable

When the Korean War began, Robert Roy was a nineteen-year-old private. On July 5, 1950, as a member of a weapons team with Task Force Smith, he discovered that his unit did not have weapons strong enough to stop the advancing North Korean tanks. His description of the ordeal is from *No Bugles, No Drums: An Oral History of the Korean War*, edited by Rudy Tomedi:

> About seven in the morning I decided to open a can of C rations [food], and that's when we saw the tanks. I just dropped the can. Nobody told us about any tanks. Before I fired the first round I counted thirty-five tanks coming down the road. From what I understand now, the South Koreans had been running from the tanks and they wanted somebody up there who wasn't going to run. We had no armor-piercing shells, so we tried to stop them by hitting the tracks [the tanks ran on]. We would've been better off throwing Molotov cocktails [gasoline bombs in bottles] at them. Some rounds were duds, some were even smoke rounds. We could see them bounce off the tanks. We fired as fast as we could. As soon as we'd get a round into the breech [of his seventy-five-millimeter recoilless rifle], we'd cover our ears and let it go, get another one in, fire that one . . . but they went right through us, right on down the road. . . . A round from one of the tanks hit right in front of my gun. I saw it coming. I saw the turret turn. We worked as fast as we could to try and get off another round, but the tank shot first, and all five of us were thrown back over the hill from the concussion and the earth hitting us in the face. Well our ears were ringing. We were all disoriented, couldn't function at all for five to ten minutes.

Korea. Its first fight came on July 5 near Osan, but even the 540 soldiers that Lt. Col. Charles B. Smith led could not stop the thirty-five tanks that attacked them. In a heart-shattering display of offensive futility, the explosive shells Smith's men fired from a variety of weapons bounced off tanks or did little damage. The rounds were not powerful enough to penetrate the metal armor that protected the tanks or were "duds" that failed to explode. Smith's men finally stopped two tanks with special high-explosive shells fired from a howitzer, an artillery piece. But when the small supply of powerful ammunition ran out, the tanks rolled through Task Force Smith's position while killing at least thirty Americans with machine gun and cannon fire.

An hour later, when the tanks approached another position, Sgt. First-Class Loran Chambers, a World War II veteran, knew he needed help. But when Chambers asked for a barrage of 60 mm mortar fire, he was told the portable cannons were too far away to hit the tanks. The rest of his conversation, as he requested help by telephone, shows how poorly equipped Task Force Smith was to deal with the Soviet tanks:

"How about some 81s [another mortar]!" he yelled.

"We don't have any."

"Hell, throw in some 4.2s [a larger mortar]!"

"We're out of that too."

"How about the artillery?"

"No communications. [A breakdown in radio contact meant soldiers could not get the help they needed.]"[39]

The T-34 Soviet tanks were, indeed, formidable—they had proven their worth in World War II by helping stop the German offensive against Moscow, the Soviet Union's capital. The T-34 was armed with machine guns and 85 mm cannons—guns that shot explosive shells—and could travel thirty-four miles an hour. The problem at the beginning of the Korean War for U.S. and ROK soldiers was that the T-34's armor—the metal skin that protected it—was so thick that none of their weapons could penetrate it to damage the tank. But U.S. forces soon had tanks that were the T-34's equal.

The Sherman Tank

The most reliable and effective of several types of UN tanks was the Sherman, which had been the U.S. Army's primary armored vehicle during World War II. Tanks travel on metal tracks instead of wheels, and the Sherman's wide tracks helped it cope with Korea's steep terrain. It could move at speeds of up to twenty-four miles per hour on open ground.

The Sherman tank's armaments included a high-velocity, 76 mm cannon, a .50-caliber heavy machine gun mounted on top of the turret (the tank's upper part), and a .30-caliber medium machine gun in its hull (body). The Sherman cannon fired high-explosive rounds and heavy antitank rounds that could pierce armor 99 mm thick at a range of one thousand meters, which was powerful enough to destroy a T-34. The Sherman itself was protected by metal plates that could withstand hits by 76 mm shells.

Although T-34s were unstoppable in the opening weeks of the invasion, UN forces began destroying them, mainly through aerial bombing. Because the North Koreans and later the Chinese had few tanks after that, tank-to-tank combat was rare. Instead, UN tanks became mobile artillery pieces and supported infantry units in combat. Soldiers sometimes rode tanks for short distances or walked behind them for protection when they headed into battle. Tanks could also drive up to enemy machine gun positions and blast them away.

An example of how tanks were used as stationary artillery comes from George Forty, who fought in Korea with the British. In *At War in Korea*, Forty explains how he and his crew prepared to support night infantry patrols: "Each evening when we brought the tank up to its firing pit, we would carefully position it in exactly the same place, using marker posts to show where the tracks should be. Having registered [set down firing coordinates] in daylight, we were able to bring

U.S. Sherman tanks were used to transport troops into battle and to counter the enemy's T-34 tanks.

down fire [on enemy positions] with pinpoint accuracy in the pitch dark and in a matter of seconds."[40]

There were some tank clashes early in the war. In October 1950, tanks fought at Ch'ongju north of Pyongyang, the North Korean capital. The following description of a tank battle on October 29 is from *Combat Actions in Korea*, a collection of U.S. Army reports:

The attack started with Lieutenant [Francis G.] Nordstrom's tank in the lead. The first shell [his tank fired] blew away some foliage that was cam-

ouflaging an enemy tank. [Nordstrom] called for armor-piercing shells and the gunner fired, hitting the front of the enemy tank from a distance of less than a hundred yards. The gunner continued firing armor-piercing shells and the third round caused a great explosion. Fire tore camouflage from a second enemy tank. Nordstorm's gunner, firing without orders, destroyed this tank with the second round. There was another violent explosion, which blew part of the enemy's tank turret [upper body] fifty feet into the air.[41]

The army had other heavy vehicles besides tanks that could transport troops into battle and provide covering fire. Armored personnel carriers like the 18.8-ton M75 ran on tracks like a tank and could carry eighteen passengers, who were protected in a boxlike superstructure. There were several types of multiple-gun motor carriages, which were basically mobile machine gun platforms. The Quad .50 was a ten-ton halftrack vehicle armed with four .50-caliber machine guns. Halftracks were equipped with a pair of wheels in front and tracks in back. The Quad was routinely used to fire up to one hundred thousand rounds per day against enemy infantry.

UN forces did not have many of these armored vehicles, but the Communists had none. They provided infantry with vital combat support. However, the two sides did fight on almost equal terms when it came to one of the most important families of weapons—artillery pieces.

Artillery

Artillery is the overall name for a wide variety of guns that hurl projectiles, usually explosive shells. Artillery has been used in warfare for many centuries, and during the Korean War it was an especially valuable weapon. Gen. Matthew B. Ridgway, who commanded UN ground forces during the conflict, once gave this family of weapons his highest praise. Said Ridgway, "Artillery has been and remains the great killer of Communists. It remains the great saver of soldiers, American and Allied. There is a direct correlation between piles of shells and piles of [our] corpses. The bigger the former, the smaller the latter."[42]

Although Ridgway's comment sounds brutal, the purpose of any weapon is to kill the enemy. Artillery pieces did their job exceedingly well in Korea, and there were many types of them. The most common was the mortar, basically a lightweight metal tube that could easily be carried into battle and that fired shells for short distances. The better-equipped UN forces also had two other short-range

Digging in Against Artillery

The last two years of the Korean War were basically fought with artillery along a static defensive line. This required UN and Communist forces to dig deep into the ground they held for protection against incoming artillery fire. In *The Korean War: History and Tactics*, David Rees explains that the differences in artillery strength of the two sides influenced the fortified positions they constructed:

Stretching [155 miles] across the peninsula of Korea the MLR's [main lines of resistance] of the two sides were fashioned for a static war that reflected their different strengths and weaknesses. The communists were forced to use the reverse slopes of the hills they held by their inferiority in [artillery] firepower. Into these reverse slopes, safe from the hands of the expertly handled UN artillery, they dug warrens [a series] of tunnels and caves to house an army of 850,000 men. . . . Their posts were constructed in a fortified belt 15 to 25 miles deep. In contrast to the Communist effort, the UN [line] was much less substantial. Because of the weight of UN firepower it took the form of a simple trench and bunker line slashed into the forward slopes of the UN-held hill crests. To provide some sort of cushion in front of the [line] itself, there were a number of fortified outposts at some distance forward of the line which made the most [for defensive purposes] of any features in the rugged Korean topography. . . . The disadvantage of the UN position was that they were so shallow. At any time a determined and sudden Chinese attack could push UN troops off [back]. . . . This situation gave rise to the numerous bloody little battles . . . which formed the only major actions of the stalemated war.

artillery pieces—the rocket launcher, better known as the bazooka, and the recoilless rifle. The Communists did not have such weapons, although they used UN pieces if they captured them.

Both sides used artillery extensively, especially in the final two years of the Korean War when UN and Communist forces fought along a static line while conducting peace talks. In *This Kind of War*, T.R. Fehrenbach notes, "Toward the end of the conflict, Korea was primarily an artillery war, with both sides dug in and cannonading each other rather than employing maneuver."[43]

Types of Artillery

Artillery is categorized by how the pieces shoot. The term *gun* refers to a long-barreled, long-range artillery piece that fires projectiles in a relatively flat trajectory. A howitzer has a shorter barrel, less range, and a moderately arched trajectory. A mortar has a very short barrel, short range, and fires at a very high angle. Since World War II, it has also been common to distinguish between light, medium, and heavy artillery. Guns and howitzers up to 105 mm in caliber are light artillery, those over 105 mm but not more than 155 mm are medium artillery, and those bigger than that are heavy artillery.

Artillery pieces can fire several types of shells: high-explosive rounds against infantry, light vehicles, and even aircraft; armor-piercing rounds to penetrate tanks and other armored vehicles; and chemical rounds that produce smoke or illumination over a battlefield. An example of how smoke rounds helped soldiers came in August 1951 during several days of fighting in the battle for Bloody Ridge. To get wounded UN soldiers to safety, artillery guns laid down a smoke screen that hid infantrymen carrying the wounded. Smoke and other shells artillery guns fired were heavy. The standard 105 mm projectile weighed about fifty pounds, the average 155 mm round was almost one hundred pounds, and the eight-inch round was nearly two hundred pounds.

Communist troops fought with the same types of artillery pieces that UN forces had. However, the North Korean and Chinese units generally had fewer big artillery pieces, and they often had trouble keeping their artillery supplied with ammunition.

Long-Range Guns

Long-range artillery like the 155 mm gun, nicknamed "Long Tom" because it had a range of fourteen miles, and the 155 mm howitzer, which could hit targets nearly eight miles away, provided long-distance support. These artillery pieces were huge—the 155 mm howitzer, which had small shields on either side of its barrel, was twenty-four feet long, weighed about 6.5 tons, and was moved by large trucks. Although these weapons were set up several miles behind combat lines, they could deliver shells with pinpoint accuracy to an area about one hundred yards in diameter.

Why Artillery Became Important in the Korean War

The last two years of the Korean War were, to a great extent, one long artillery battle. Artillery had been important in the war even before the two sides established static defensive lines in the summer of 1951. But afterward, both sides placed an even greater importance on such weapons. In "Ammunition in the Korean War," an analysis posted on the U.S. Army Logistics Management College website, Capt. David A. Martin explains why artillery came to the fore in this conflict:

> Artillery is sometimes called the "King of Battle." Never was that nickname more deserved than during the Korean War. Several factors were responsible for the important role artillery assumed in the Korean War. Rapid maneuver during the opening months of the conflict soon gave way to stalemate, somewhat like that experienced in World War I. As a result, during the last two years of the Korean War, while the truce talks at Panmunjom progressed at a glacial pace, U.S. commanders relied on artillery to do the lion's share of the fighting: interdicting enemy movements, responding to enemy batteries, and countering enemy offensive actions. The beginning of the truce talks led to a change in battlefield tactics, with the artillery barrage replacing the hill assault as the primary battlefield activity. The number of artillery pieces increased during the course

of the war, which, of course, led to greater demands for ammunition. The conflict evolved into a contest between manpower and firepower . . . as commanders sought to overcome an 8:1 Communist manpower advantage through a 100:1 [United Nations] UN firepower advantage.

U.S. Marines stand armed in a trench just two hundred yards from enemy soldiers.

The big guns attacked soldiers and fortified positions, especially artillery emplacements. They were often the saviors of the infantry because they could slow down or stop attacking enemy forces.

The guns were serviced by crews of a dozen or more soldiers who had to perform many different types of jobs besides just firing them. One of the most important tasks was to communicate with soldiers

"Long Tom" 155 mm guns fire long-range artillery shells several miles into enemy positions.

in the field, called forward observers, so gun crews would know exactly where to place their shells; if the artillery pieces were off target, they could hit their own men with "friendly fire." Artillerymen also had to maintain the weapons and even put shells together before they could fire them. Nick Tosques, who served with the 555th Field Artillery, explains this job:

You had the shell, and then you had the shell casing [which contained the explosive to fire the shell]. Inside each casing there were nine powder bags. The range of a 105 mm howitzer was seven-and-half miles, and if all nine bags were in there the shell went seven-and-a-half miles. If the forward observer called for a shorter range, you put in fewer bags. I learned how to load the gun, I learned how to fire it, and I learned everything fast, because if you didn't, you didn't survive.[44]

For most of the war, UN forces enjoyed an advantage in artillery, especially in big guns and howitzers. In an analysis of artillery use in the Korean War, Capt. David A. Martin writes that this was key to countering an enemy who usually had more soldiers: "Throughout the Korean War, senior commanders like [Gen. Matthew B.] Ridgway sought to offset the huge Communist manpower advantage through the use of artillery and firepower."[45]

Mortars

When it came to mortars, however, the Communists fought on equal terms with UN soldiers. The mortar was a simple sealed-breech tube mounted on a heavy base plate and supported by rods extending to the side. Although one soldier could fire a mortar, two-man teams usually operated them. UN forces had 60 mm, 81 mm, and 4.2-inch mortars. Both sides used mortars to attack enemy soldiers and to destroy gun emplacements and other fortified positions.

The Communists relied heavily on mortars because they were cheap to make and could be easily transported by their armies, which had few motorized vehicles. Communist mortars fired 61 mm, 82 mm, and 120 mm shells. Because their bore was slightly larger, the Communist 82 mm and 61 mm mortars could fire American 81 mm and 60 mm shells. This

Land Mines

Another weapon that both sides used in the Korean War was the land mine. These deadly explosive devices, undetectable when buried in the ground, killed thousands of soldiers who accidentally walked on them, triggering the weapons. A variation of the standard land mine was the *fougasse,* a fifty-five-gallon drum filled with napalm and explosives that was also buried in the ground. *Combat Support in Korea,* edited by John G. Westover, is a collection of oral recollections on how various support units helped the infantry. In the fall of 1950, Maj. David F. Campbell was a military adviser who helped guide Republic of Korea soldiers who laid mines for defensive purposes around the Naktong Perimeter. He explains how well the mines worked in one situation:

As our infantry withdrew down the Yodok-tong road toward Hill 728, the enemy attacked banzai style and a regiment strong, through Minefields 2 and 3. These minefields had been built up to contain some five hundred antipersonnel mines, and we had them covered with small arms fire. Rifle and machine-gun fire did not stop the enemy, but the mines stopped them cold. They milled around for a few moments trying to find a passage [through the mines] . . . the attack soon stopped and our men withdrew without further interference.

However, Sam Starobin, who laid mines with the army's Sixth Engineer Combat Battalion, soon realized that mines could be dangerous to soldiers on both sides:

Mines are double-edged weapons. Properly employed they can be a strong instrument of defense. Improperly used they are a menace. Especially is this true for an Army like ours, where vast numbers of trucks and tanks are employed. I have seen at least 150 disabled North Korean tanks—none of which had been destroyed by mines. I have also seen a great number of American tanks and tracks destroyed by our own mines. Not all of these were in minefields laid by Americans. A large percentage of the mines that destroyed our vehicles and killed our troops had been re-laid by the enemy.

was a huge advantage for the Communists, enabling them to use UN shells while UN troops could not do the same with their larger rounds.

Mortars fired shells at a high trajectory. This made them perfect for combat in Korea, where the mountainous landscape was dominated by high ridges and hills that soldiers could hide behind. In a report for the U.S. Army on weapons use in the Korean War, S.L.A. Marshall, then a soldier himself, explained why this weapon became so important: "Korea—being an unending complex of steep hills and sharp-faced ridges—is natural mortar country."[46]

Mortars were easy to carry and fire. For example, the U.S. 81 mm mortar was less than four feet in length and weighed 136 pounds assembled. It had a maximum range of 3,290 yards—soldiers altered the range by changing the mortar tube's angle—and could fire between eighteen and thirty rounds per minute. Soldiers dropped shells in and fired them by pressing an electric ignition switch.

The only complaint soldiers had about mortars was that the base plate they rested on often cracked in the severe cold of the Korean winter. Despite this minor problem, Marshall explains that soldiers depended on them heavily. Commenting on the 4.2, a new, more powerful mortar that debuted in Korea, Marshall wrote,

This weapon is the workhorse of infantry operations in Korea. None of the other relatively new weapons has

been put to more general usage or found greater favor among troops. The enthusiasm for it is unanimous. The 4.2 is accurate and sturdy; the round packs as much wallop as a 105 mm shell; for continuity of performance, and visible impact upon an emergency situation, it is valued more highly than any other weapon within the infantry regiment.[47]

Bazookas and Recoilless Rifles

Included in the artillery family are two weapons that infantry soldiers carried into combat—the bazooka and the recoilless rifle. One of them, however, was a failure in the first few weeks of the war. When members of Task Force Smith used the bazooka on T-34s, the 2.36-inch shell it fired did little damage to tanks. Complained one soldier, "These damn bazookas don't do any good against those heavy tanks. They just bounce off."[48] This problem was remedied when the army sent new, more powerful bazookas, which fired a 3.5-inch shell strong enough to destroy tanks.

Basically a long, narrow tube, the bazooka weighed just under sixteen pounds. It was sixty-one inches long when assembled but only twenty-one inches long when it was taken apart, making it easy to carry. The bazooka could fire an explosive shell on a flat trajectory up to 400 yards, and at 120 yards the shell could punch through tank armor. In addition to destroy-

A UN mortar crew is barricaded behind stacks of ammunition castings after repelling the advance of nearly twenty thousand Communist troops.

ing armored vehicles, the bazooka was used against machine gun emplacements and other enemy positions. To escape backblast from the bazooka when it was fired, the soldier using it held the bazooka on his shoulder, with about half the tube extending behind him.

A 3.5 bazooka proved valuable during a Chinese attack in November 1950 at Hagaru-ri. Col. R.L. Murray, commander of the Fifth Regiment, explained how the weapon helped destroy a mortar emplacement: "Sgt. Paul West, with a 3.5 [rocket]

launcher in his lap [had] been watching the action, but so far had taken no part in it. So he raised the launcher and let go one rocket. His first round hit the Chinese mortar dead on—at 225 yards range. That cooled off the enemy force attacking up the draw. When the mortar and crew were knocked out, their machine gun went silent."[49]

Recoilless rifles, which came in 57 mm, 75 mm, and 106 mm calibers, were infantry weapons that fired conventional artillery shells along a flat trajectory. Like the bazooka, the recoilless rifle was designed as an antitank weapon, but in Korea it was also effective against troops and fortifications. Recoilless rifles were harder to carry than bazookas—the 106 mm rifle was about eleven feet long and weighed about 250 pounds, minus its firing tripod—but they had a range of up to eleven hundred yards. Two-man crews could fire about five rounds per minute.

In late 1950 George Zonge was in charge of a weapons platoon with the army's Third Infantry Division. In the battle for the Chosin Reservoir, he and his men used recoilless rifles:

Being in a weapons platoon, mostly I was up on the ridges to support the infantry down on the roads. A 57 mm recoilless rifle is really a small can-

An American soldier fires a 75 mm rocket launcher as his fellow infantrymen protect their ears.

non, but it's light enough for a man to carry. It's got a range of about seven hundred yards, and my boys were good. They [infantry units] were always calling on us. We'd blow the Chinese out of caves in the hills. We'd shoot up their roadblocks.[50]

Machine Guns

In addition to the lightweight machine guns that infantry soldiers carried into battle, heavier, more powerful machine guns were fired from fixed positions or mounted on trucks, tanks, and other vehicles. These weapons were so powerful that they were usually operated by two-man teams, and they had high rates of fire; the UN .50-caliber heavy machine gun, for example, fired 575 rounds per minute to a range of two thousand yards. The Communists also had bigger machine guns. One of their favorites was the Soviet Goryunov heavy machine gun, which was usually mounted on a small base with wheels and was pulled manually.

These big machine guns weighed eighty pounds or more, making them too heavy for mobile combat. Although they were so big that two soldiers normally operated them off a metal base, in emergencies one

The devastating power of flamethrowers offered UN forces an advantage over Communist troops.

soldier, if he was strong enough, could lift and fire one. In December 1950, while defending a position at Chosin Reservoir, one soldier had no choice but to do just that. An army action report on the incident states, "As one enemy group climbed a steep ridge toward a heavy machine gun operated by Cpl. Robert Lee Armentrout, the corporal discovered he could not depress his gun enough [lower the trajectory of bullets] to hit the enemy.

He then picked up his weapon, tripod and all, cradled it in his arms, and beat off the attack."[51]

Flamethrowers

UN troops also fought with flamethrowers, which the Communists did not have. It was a fearsome weapon, one that could shoot a sheet of flame fifty yards.

The soldier operating the flamethrower wore a backpack with three cylinder tanks; the two outside tanks held a flammable oil-based liquid fuel, and the middle one contained a flammable compressed gas, such as butane. When the operator squeezed the trigger, the gas and liquid fuel came together; the pressurized gas then expelled it outward past an ignition system, usually an electric current. The flame could travel fifty yards, but the weapons only had enough fuel for about eight seconds of continuous flame. Some tanks were also equipped with bigger, more powerful flamethrowers.

Army lieutenant colonel William C. Hammond Jr. claimed the flamethrower became a potent weapon in Korea because it could scare enemy soldiers. He explains the reaction of some North Korean soldiers during one battle when a flamethrower was fired at them: "The enemy fears fire. [One time] a tank went into a valley and fired one burst of flame. For a distance of a thousand yards all the enemy ducked down into their holes and stopped firing—including those way up on the sides of hills whom we could not possibly have reached. The psychological factor was tremendous."[52]

The Lack of Weapons Hurts

Although UN forces generally had many more specialized weapons than the Communists, their lack of them hurt during the Korean War's opening weeks. Col. Carl Bernard won a Distinguished Service Cross for his heroic actions on July 11, 1950, when he and another soldier disabled two tanks while armed only with rifles.

When Bernard received the medal, he sent it back to his superiors with an angry note saying it should have been given to the men in his unit who were killed or captured that day. Bernard blamed these casualties on the fact that his unit did not have decent weapons to fight the tanks. Said Bernard, "I lost nearly 101 men killed or captured out of a rifle company of 130 people. Thirty-three men died in captivity. When [my] company got down to fighting tanks, I [realized] our bazookas didn't work. The seat in hell closest to the fire is reserved for the Army officers who knew this and didn't tell me."[53]

But UN forces generally did have the weapons they needed in such situations. And those tanks, howitzers, bazookas, and flamethrowers ensured that a lot fewer of those soldiers would die in combat.

Chapter 4

Aerial Warfare in the Korean War

From June 27, 1950, to July 27, 1953, United Nations aircraft flew more than 1,040,708 sorties in pursuit of three main objectives—achieving air superiority, supporting ground troops during combat, and weakening Communist forces through strategic bombing. *Sortie* is a military term that refers to one trip by one plane for any reason, from a bombing raid to a delivery of supplies.

During their more than 1 million missions, UN pilots dropped nearly seven hundred thousand tons of ordnance—a military term for bombs, napalm, and other explosives—and fired over 200 million machine gun bullets. The list of targets they destroyed included 976 airplanes and more than 1,300 tanks, 960 train locomotives, 1,100 bridges, 118,000 buildings, and 8,600 artillery positions. Air crews also estimated that they killed more than 185,000 soldiers.

From the very first days of the conflict, UN planes controlled the skies over North and South Korea. Robert F. Futrell,

author of an official history of the U.S. Air Force during the Korean War, claims UN air supremacy gave a huge boost to the overall war effort: "The early accomplishment of United Nations Command air superiority paid large dividends. Without hazard of hostile air attack, United Nations surface forces could maneuver freely by day to resist the more powerful Communist [ground] forces."[54]

UN Air Superiority

When North Korea attacked South Korea on June 25, 1950, it had 132 planes at airfields near Pyongyang, its capital, and Yonpo on its eastern coast. The aircraft, all propeller-driven planes manufactured by the Soviet Union, included 70 Yak fighters, 22 Yak transports, and 8 small training aircraft.

Despite the relative weakness of this small fleet, it was impressive in comparison to the handful of light planes South Korea had. A North Korean pilot shot down on

June 29 admitted that this discrepancy in air power had been a factor in launching the war: "Soviet advisors have ordered us to bomb South Korea because they know for sure the South Koreans have very few planes and only small ones."[55]

But when the United Nations came to South Korea's defense, the tiny North Korean air force suddenly found itself facing the world's greatest air power—the United States. Although pilots from other UN countries, such as Great Britain, flew missions, they accounted for fewer than forty-five thousand UN sorties.

The UN air command consisted mostly of planes and pilots from the air force, the aviation branch of America's military, and the navy and marines.

The aerial matchup proved disastrous for North Korea. President Harry S. Truman immediately authorized the air force to help beleaguered South Korea, and on June 27 five F-82 Mustangs engaged five Yak-11 fighters. In the war's first aerial combat, Lt. William G. Hudson and radar operator Lt. Carl Fraser drew first blood by shooting down a Yak-11 fighter. This first UN victory set the tone for the rest of the conflict.

U.S. planes were superior to the North Korean aircraft they faced and so were their pilots, mainly because their World War II combat experience made them better fighters. UN bombers began destroying North Korean planes sitting unpro-

tected on the ground, and fighters shot down more planes in aerial combat. Historian Anthony Robinson notes that within a few weeks "the North Korean Air Force had virtually ceased to exist."[56]

Fighter Planes

Most of the planes that the U.S. Air Force flew in the war were the same propeller-driven aircraft that had helped America win World War II. In Korea, however, the United States also had several jet fighters, a plane with a new, much more powerful

U.S. Air Force F-86 Sabre jet fighters are readied for combat. The Korean War was the first in which jet planes played a major role.

type of engine that enabled it to fly farther faster. Instead of a conventional motor that turned a propeller, a jet had an engine that produced a stream of pressurized air to make it fly.

Fighter planes are small, fast, heavily armed aircraft—their armaments can include machine guns, rockets, cannons, and bombs—that attack other planes, support ground troops, and strike ground targets. The F-86 was much faster than jets built just a few years earlier—its top speed was over seven hundred miles per hour—and far more maneuverable.

The Korean War was the first in which jet planes played a major role. The F-86 Sabre—the *F* stood for "Fighter"—became famous for opening the age of jet warfare in Korea, where its sole mission was to battle the Soviet-built MiG-15. The MiG, a jet perfected and manufactured by the Soviet Union, saw extensive action in the Korean War.

However, two older U.S. jets—the F-80 Shooting Star and F-84 Thunderjet— proved valuable in other ways. The F-80, which could fly nearly six hundred miles an hour and was the air force's first operational jet fighter, provided ground combat support with machine gun fire and low-level rocket, bomb, and napalm attacks. The F-84 was used on similar missions as well as to bomb targets like airfields and dams.

The U.S. military had several prop-driven fighter planes that were also potent weapons. Two air force fighters of this genre were the F-51 Mustang and F-82 Mustang; the navy and marines flew fighters like the Panther and Corsair.

The F-51 was one of the best of the older fighters. It had a wingspan of thirty-seven feet, was thirty-two feet long, and was twelve feet high; it had a top speed of 437 miles per hour and a cruising range of one thousand miles. It had been considered one of the great airplanes of World War II; Hermann Göring, who headed the German *Luftwaffe* (air force), once remarked, "When I saw the Mustangs over Berlin, I knew that the air war was lost."[57] Even in an age of speedy jets like the F-86, the F-51 and other prop-driven fighters were mighty weapons.

Bombers

Bombers were also used in the conflict. These large planes, capable of carrying many tons of bombs, flew missions against strategic targets such as bridges, hydroelectric plants, railroad tracks, troop and supply truck convoys, and concentrations of enemy soldiers. These planes were flown exclusively by U.S. Air Force pilots; the Communists never used them.

Bombers included the B-26 Invader, which conducted the first bombing missions of the war; based in nearby Japan, they were quickly sent into combat when the conflict began. Just four days after fighting started, B-26s bombed the Pyongyang airfield, destroying twenty-five enemy planes. B-26s took to the skies fifty-five thousand times during the Korean War.

The F-51 Mustang Gets a Locomotive

Although the F-51 Mustang vintage fighter plane had been one of the best flying in World War II, it was outdated in the Korean War in comparison to jets like the F-86 Sabre. In *Hotshots: An Oral History of the Air Force Combat Pilots of the Korean War*, edited by Jennie Ethell Chancey and William R. Forstchen, Lt. Duane E. Biteman remarks that pilots loved the F-51 even though it was an older plane. He explains how he flew one to destroy a locomotive engine:

I found four trucks heading out of Pyongyang [the North Korean capital] and was able to destroy them all with just my machine guns, saving my rockets for something more lucrative. And a prize it was: a locomotive [the car that pulls a train] with a half dozen boxcars about to enter a short mountain tunnel. There was little room to maneuver in the narrow canyon, but as I dove to intercept I knew that I could get a fairly straight shot into the tunnel from the far side by flying down the railroad approach, then pulling up at the last instant to just clear the hills above—and that's just what I did. I got a beautiful rocket launch right into the tunnel to destroy the locomotive.

U.S. Air Force F-51 Mustangs are loaded with rockets at a UN base in Korea.

The war's workhorse bomber, however, was the B-29 Superfortress, a larger plane that carried much heavier bomb loads. B-29s flew all but twenty-one days of the war, dropping 167,000 tons of bombs in twenty-one thousand sorties; its crews also shot down sixteen MiGs and seventeen other fighters. Most of the B-29s saw action only after the air force took them out of storage and refurbished them.

The B-29 was massive—99 feet long, nearly 30 feet tall, and its wings stretched more than 141 feet—and its range of fifty-six hundred miles enabled it to engage in long-distance missions while carrying up to twenty thousand pounds of ordnance. It took several airmen to handle the plane, including a pilot, copilot, navigator, bombardier who released the bombs, and several gunners who fired .50-caliber machine guns mounted on several parts of the plane. The plane is most famous for two missions in August 1945, when B-29s dropped atomic bombs on the Japanese cities of Hiroshima and Nagasaki to end World War II.

Although the B-29 could defend itself with machine guns, the slow-moving bomber—its top speed was 357 miles per hour, and its cruising speed was only 220 miles per hour—was an easy target for a MiG-15, which could fly twice as fast. First Lt. E.J. McGill, who piloted a B-29, remembers how vulnerable his big, lumbering plane was when a MiG attacked it: "This MiG went right through our formation. Then, he stalled out. His nose pointed up. Everybody fired at him. Our top gun opened up. Our bombardier was onto him, blazing away. Nobody got him. The MiG lost altitude, recovered and flew away."[58]

Until the MiGs showed up in October 1950, after China entered the war, B-29s and other UN aircraft had operated with little or no resistance. But the MiG-15s began to knock B-29s out of the sky with ease. On what is known as Black Tuesday, October 23, 1951, nine B-29s were flying on a mission to bomb Namsi, which was located along the Yalu River. MiG planes shot down three B-29s and damaged several others, forcing them to turn back. The casualties that day—twenty-eight airmen killed and twenty-four wounded—were the largest the air force suffered in any single day of the war.

Air force officials decided the MiGs made it too dangerous for their bombers to operate during daylight hours. Bombers began attacking at night, when the MiGs had trouble locating them. Also, because MiGs flew only in northwest North Korea near their bases across the Yalu River in China, their effect on UN air power was limited.

The air force did have one jet-powered bomber—the B-45 Tornado. However, there were only a few of them available, and they were used for night reconnaissance.

Other Aircraft

The air force had planes designed to accomplish many types of tasks. The biggest were cargo aircraft like the C-54 Skymaster, which had the dubious distinction of being the first U.S. aircraft destroyed in the conflict—one was strafed while parked on an airfield by enemy planes firing machine guns and rockets the day the war began; the C-47 Skytrain, nicknamed the "Gooney Bird"; and the C-119 Flying Boxcar. As an example of their size, the C-54 was 117 feet long, almost 94 feet high, and weighed 62,000 pounds; it had a top speed of only 265 miles per hour but a range of 3,900 miles.

These aerial behemoths hauled supplies, evacuated wounded soldiers, and ferried paratroopers, soldiers who parachuted into battle. The big planes could carry trucks and other huge pieces of equipment, delivering them either by landing or dropping them from the air via parachutes. One of the war's most dramatic airlifts was in December 1950 when C-119s delivered a prefabricated bridge to the First Marine Division, which was about to be overwhelmed by Chinese soldiers. Each bridge section the planes dropped weighed two tons. The Marine Corps used the sections to build a bridge so they could cross a gorge fifteen hundred feet deep and escape the advancing Chinese.

The air force, navy, and marines also flew many smaller planes, mainly for reconnaissance missions to find out information about the enemy, such as where Communist troops were located and how many soldiers there were. One mission was to photograph enemy positions. Capt. Cass J. Joswiak remembers that the pictures he took from a small plane "showed where to expect trouble from the enemy and provided accurate views of the terrain."[59]

Small planes like the air force AT-6 Texan were also used to guide bombers and fighter planes providing close support to ground troops. The small AT-6 carried a pilot and a spotter, who hunted positions of enemy troops and weapons; the pilot then fired smoke rockets to guide the big planes to the target. These so-called mosquito missions were dangerous because the small planes had to fly low and slow, exposing them to enemy ground fire. But these risky flights were vital to one of the UN's main aerial tasks—providing close support for troops in combat.

Close Support

In close support, airmen helped the infantry fighting far below them by attack-

Shedding Light on the Enemy

UN bombing missions in the Korean War were often conducted at night. The problem was that the same darkness that protected the big bombers from attack by smaller, faster MiG-15 jet fighters also made it hard for air crews to see their targets. In *The United States Air Force in Korea, 1950–1953*, an official history written for that branch of the military, author Robert F. Futrell explains two of the innovative ways air crews illuminated targets:

On 11 September [1950] General [George E.] Stratemeyer had directed the Fifth Air Force and Bomber Command to conduct joint experimental missions in cooperative night attacks against moving targets. Under this "buddy" system a B-29, loaded with 100 parachute flares (paraflares) set to ignite at 6,000 feet, orbited above a previously arranged point over a communications artery on which the light bombers wished to attack moving traffic. When the B-29 crew lighted the target area with flares, the slow-flying B-26 attacked the Communists with bombs and machine guns.

A team of U.S. Air Force B-29 Superfortresses releases tons of bombs onto a strategic North Korean target.

ing and weakening opposing ground forces. This included bombing and strafing enemy soldiers, destroying tanks, and knocking out artillery guns. Planes also airlifted supplies, something that was vital when soldiers were surrounded by the enemy and there was no other way to deliver necessities like food and ammunition.

Such aerial combat support played a key role in the first few weeks of the con-

flict, when UN forces were being overwhelmed by larger numbers of North Koreans. An example of this occurred on July 10 when F-80s, B-26s, and F-82s destroyed 117 trucks, 38 tanks, and 7 other armored vehicles near Pyongtaek, South Korea. The attack weakened North Korea's single armored division, making it easier for UN forces to withstand enemy attacks and hold the precarious defensive position known as the Pusan Perimeter.

Despite the rivalry that has always existed between the different branches of the U.S. military, Gen. Walton H. Walker gratefully admitted that the air force helped his Eighth Army avoid being defeated: "I will gladly lay my cards right on the table and state that, if it had not been for the air support that we received from the Fifth Air Force, we would not have been able to stay in Korea."[60]

The UN bombing of enemy troops early in the war that was part of this close support was so severe and so successful that it even made the North Koreans change their tactics. Duane E. Biteman, who was a lieutenant when he piloted a bomber during the summer of 1950, claims,

The impact of our repeated daylight fighter attacks [in support of ground troops] became apparent rather suddenly during the last week in July. Where the [Communists] had previously charged blindly ahead in full daylight—seemingly oblivious to the toll we were taking on their tanks, trucks, and troops—they suddenly began seeking concealment during the day, making their advances only at night [a situation that continued throughout the war].[61]

The Communists had to begin playing a deadly game of hide-and-seek. They would camouflage themselves and their weapons so that UN planes could not find and destroy them. Lt. Wun Hong Ki, a captured tank officer, explains how this worked: "We always moved at night, but found that UN air would attack groves [of trees] and orchards even though tanks could not be seen. So profiting from the experience of others, we put tanks in buildings or destroyed villages where they could be easily camouflaged."[62]

When the positions of enemy and friendly soldiers were close together, often only hundreds of yards separated them, providing close support was difficult. And sometimes, mistakes happened. Arnold Winter was a Marine Corps private trying to hold the Pusan Perimeter when navy Corsairs provided close support. "We would throw our flags for the Corsair pilots, and they would come in and strafe [Communist positions] right up to the red flags," Winter said. "But sometimes they'd screw up and shoot our own guys."[63]

Such tragic incidents are known as friendly fire, but they happened only occasionally. More often the support saved UN lives, as in August 1951 when four fighter planes dropped napalm bombs on Bloody Ridge, a hill the Ninth Infantry Regiment was desperately trying to defend against a Chinese attack. A U.S. Army battle report explains the attack's efficiency: "[The bombs] fell so close the men could feel the heat from the burning napalm. The infantrymen, watching the fire mushroom [over the Communist position] turn from orange to black, cheered and shouted."[64]

Napalm and Rockets

When older U.S. fighter planes like the F-80 Shooting Star engaged in close-support missions, they were often outfitted with rockets, a short-range explosive missile they fired directly at their targets, and sometimes carried a new weapon called napalm. Napalm is a jellied form of petroleum that burns fiercely when it explodes and sticks to anything it hits. In *Top Guns: America's Fighter Aces Tell Their Stories* by legendary World War II ace Joe Foss and Matthew Brennan, Capt. Harold Fischer explains that these types of ordnance were more difficult to deliver than a regular bomb, which could easily be dropped when he was over the target.

Fischer explains the procedure for dropping napalm:

> The pilot would get down as low as possible, usually less than fifty feet [from the ground]. When the target disappeared under the nose of the aircraft, the napalm would be released—both tanks at once, or one at a time for better coverage. According to reports from prisoners of war, napalm was the most feared weapon we had, and it was impossible to miss with it [because it spread out over a large area].

Fischer also said it was much harder to aim and fire rockets, a weapon he did not have much faith in anyway because of the difficulty in using them. This is how Fischer said he fired rockets:

> Rocketry was more difficult. In order to be effective, it was necessary to get almost a direct hit, and since the launching technique was from 3,000 feet at an angle of thirty to forty-five degrees, many factors entered into a successful launch. Our gunsights had a setting for rocketry, but most pilots estimated the correct range and altitude and, in many cases, the attack was about as successful as throwing rocks at the enemy.

An F-51 Mustang drops napalm canisters over a North Korean town.

Air Interdiction

UN planes also protected troops with a deadly bombing campaign aimed at destroying enemy soldiers, supplies, and equipment before the troops or matériel reached the battlefield. This tactic was called interdiction. The massive daily bombing was a twin operation—the air force struck targets in the west from air bases located there, and the navy hit objectives in the east, often with planes launched from aircraft carriers floating off the Korean coast.

Interdiction missions tried to sever supply lines so Communist soldiers could not receive needed supplies. Air force general Hoyt S. Vandenberg said such "air attacks have been compared to the cavalry of the [U.S.] Civil War, which often disrupted supply lines for only brief periods."[65] Vandenberg also claimed that military experts had learned an important lesson in the century-old war that had almost divided America forever— that to be successful, an army had to attack supply lines constantly. Bob Ennis, who flew a B-26 Invader, says UN planes did just that: "A single B-26 would go out and over a particular stretch of highway or railroad. But between our two bomb wings we covered every road and railroad in Korea. Every road and railroad would have an airplane over it every night."[66]

To stop transportation of war supplies, planes destroyed long sections of highway and railroad track and hunted trains and truck convoys. Locomotives, the engines that pulled trains, were a prized target. Pilots who destroyed five locomotives won the title of "locomotive ace," a variation of the designation *ace* given to combat pilots who downed five planes.

Although bombing missions destroyed an estimated 90 percent of the Communist truck and rail transport system, they never completely stopped the flow of supplies. So, in addition to continuing to attack supply lines, UN planes also began striking other targets to weaken North Korea. In June 1952 planes began raiding hydroelectric generating plants. As a result, North Korea experienced a nearly total loss of electric power for two weeks, and it never regained the same level of generating capacity until after the war ended.

The incessant heavy bombing also destroyed villages, rice fields, and many other areas in both Koreas. In 1951, when Gen. Douglas MacArthur testified before Congress after President Harry S. Truman had dismissed him, he admitted the damage that had already been done was so bad that it sickened even a veteran soldier such as himself: "The war in Korea has almost destroyed that nation. I have never seen such devastation. I have seen, I guess, as much blood and disaster as any living man, and it just curdled my stomach the last time I was there."[67]

Helicopters

One type of aircraft, however, helped alleviate suffering—helicopters, which made their military debut in the Korean War. Helicopters are most famous for taking wounded soldiers to hospitals, enabling them to receive medical help more quickly than in any other war.

But the helicopters that navy and air force pilots flew in Korea also performed a wide variety of combat roles. Helicopters were able to land quickly and easily almost anywhere, which suited them for rescuing airmen when their planes were shot down behind enemy lines or in the sea and delivering supplies or flying soldiers into combat in remote areas. They were also used to scout enemy positions and transport heavy objects, such as rocket launchers.

Marine lieutenant James Brady remembers how impressed he was with the strange new aircraft, which soldiers nicknamed "chopper" because of the noise its whirling rotor blades made. Brady was a passenger once when his unit was airlifted into a combat zone: "We were getting some incoming mortar fire when the helicopters brought us in on the reverse slopes of the new hill called 880. The choppers were coming in every half minute now. This was pretty big stuff to us, only the second time an entire battalion had moved into [combat] by helicopter."[68]

A wounded U.S. Marine is carried to a helicopter. Helicopters made their military debut in Korea.

Although a few helicopters were equipped with rocket launchers, thus turning them into offensive weapons, their main mission was carrying wounded soldiers. Lt. Martin Blumenson explains how grateful the infantry was for helicopters: "The presence of helicopters in Korea helped morale."[69] Just how well the helicopter justified such confidence can be seen from this statistic: In World War II, forty-five out of every one thousand wounded who reached the hospital later died; but, in the Korean War, thanks in no small part to getting there quicker via helicopter, only twenty-five out of each one thousand succumbed to their wounds.

Flying Was Dangerous

Even though helicopters saved the lives of many pilots, flying was dangerous, and many Korean War airmen were wounded and died. The air force alone suffered 1,144 airmen killed and 306 wounded. Although some planes crashed due to mechanical problems or bad weather, the biggest risk airmen faced was being shot down by other planes or by antiaircraft guns. In early 1953 the latter almost killed John Glenn, a future astronaut and U.S. senator who was then a young Marine Corps lieutenant.

When Glenn first got to Korea, he piloted an F9F Panther, and he quickly discovered how dangerous flying could be. After making two runs to destroy an anti-aircraft gun emplacement over Sinanju, he flew back to his base near Seoul. When Glenn got out and inspected his plane, he was shocked at what he found: "[A] hole in the Panther's tail that was big enough to put my head and shoulders through. There were another 250 smaller shrapnel holes around the big one. We figured it was a thirty-seven millimeter shell that hit me; a larger one would have blown the tail off. Crews replaced the tail and the Panther flew as good as new."[70]

Pilots called antiaircraft fire "flak," and the explosive shells from those guns were deadly. F-84 pilot Lt. Jay Brentlinger estimates that more shots were fired at him on just one mission than were fired at the average foot soldier in an entire year. Navy pilot Jim Service remembers how strange this enemy fire looked:

The first time I saw flak I didn't even realize what I was looking at. I thought to myself: God, all those funny little white clouds are sure in a strange place. Then I saw some big black clouds, really angry-looking ones, and I thought: Hey, I know what *this* is. Each cloud represented an explosion, of course, the flak shells bursting in the air. Many times you'd fly a mission over a target where you'd see hundreds of these little clouds blossoming all over the sky. Any one of them could knock your airplane down, but you were simply too busy flying the aircraft to worry about getting hit.[71]

During the war, UN forces lost 1,041 aircraft to enemy action—147 in air-to-air combat, 816 to ground fire, and 78 to unknown enemy action. Although this total is higher than the number of enemy planes UN forces destroyed (960), it was a minuscule percentage of the huge number of aircraft it sent into the air each and every day.

Bedcheck Charlie

The David-versus-Goliath nature of air power in the Korean War is symbolized by the only sustained aerial offense the North Korean air force was able to conduct. And that was the annoying night-time flights of small, slow Soviet planes flown by pilots whom UN soldiers nicknamed "Bedcheck Charlie" because they always came late at night and woke them

A Brave Helicopter Pilot

During the Korean War, the helicopter was far more than an aerial ambulance. One helicopter pilot, navy lieutenant John Kelvin Koelsch, won the Medal of Honor for his daring attempt on July 3, 1951, to rescue a downed Marine Corps pilot west of Kosong, North Korea. The story of his heroic flight is from "Valor in the Forgotten War," an article by Hill Goodspeed on the U.S. Naval Historical Center website:

Gathering darkness and thick overcast precluded fighter escort for the slow, vulnerable helicopter, so Koelsch and his crewman, George M. Neal, proceeded alone. Having bailed out of his Corsair [fighter] after being hit by ground fire, Captain James V. Wilkins had landed in a valley and begun to make his way up the slope of a mountain when he heard the "whop-whop-whop" of a helicopter. Reversing course, he descended into the valley just as Koelsch's [helicopter] passed over the area at 50 feet altitude amid intense ground fire. Wilkins thought the helicopter pilot would immediately leave the area, but Koelsch returned to the valley despite having his aircraft rocked by a near miss. To the Marine aviator on the ground "it was the greatest display of guts I've ever seen." Positioning his helicopter over Wilkins, Koelsch instructed Neal to lower the rescue sling. The downed pilot got into it and was raised about three feet off the ground when a North Korean shell struck home, sending the [helicopter] down in flames.

Goodspeed explains that although Wilkins was burned on both legs and had a twisted knee, the trio got away. However, they were captured a week later and imprisoned. When the war ended, Neal and Wilkins were released as prisoners of war. Koelsch, however, had died in captivity, where, Goodspeed writes, "he resisted his captors and provided aid to his fellow prisoners [until his death from malnutrition and the disease dysentery]." On August 1, 1955, Koelsch was posthumously awarded the Medal of Honor—the first helicopter pilot to receive his nation's highest honor.

up. The North Korean pilots would fire a few machine gun bullets or drop a couple of small bombs, but generally they did very little damage.

The light planes flew so slowly that the much faster jet fighters had trouble engaging them in combat. When nighttime attacks escalated on the Kimpo air base near Seoul, navy pilots in older Corsair fighters were brought in. The Corsairs flew more slowly, which made it easier for them to battle the Communist aircraft. On July 1, 1951, Lt. Guy Bordelon shot down his first plane. During the next two weeks Bordelon shot down four more to become the first "Bedcheck Charlie" ace. Bordelon was the only navy pilot to achieve the status of ace for downing five enemy planes, even if they were slow and old Bedcheck Charlies.

Such encounters typified the aviation war in Korea. It was an aerial battle that, for the most part, pitted a few small, antiquated planes against a host of magnificent flying machines. It was a war the UN easily won from the very first day.

Chapter 5

The Age of Jet Fighter Warfare Begins

The Korean War's most dramatic weapons innovation was that jet airplanes, which climbed higher and traveled faster than any aircraft that had ever flown, clashed for the first time in individual combat. In these deadly aerial duels, two opponents sparred in a dramatic life-or-death tactical ballet tens of thousands of feet above the earth at speeds of six hundred miles per hour.

Some of the war's biggest heroes were jet pilots who achieved the heralded status of ace, a pilot who had shot down at least five enemy planes; there were forty American aces in the Korean War, thirty-eight from the air force and one each from the navy and marines. Air force captain Joseph McConnell was the leading ace with 16 "kills," more victories than any other pilot in the conflict, and all of them over MiG-15s. He was followed closely by Maj. James Jabara, with 15, and Capt. Manuel J. Fernandez, with 14.5 (a half-kill was registered when two pilots combined to down a plane).

McConnell's first kill came in the fall of 1952, and in just over a month he shot down four more planes to become the air force's twenty-seventh ace. His last aerial victory came on January 14, 1953. On that day the pilots of four Communist jet fighters tried to trick him with the "hit and run," a maneuver in which two planes would attack a lone plane and try to get it to chase them while two others moved into position behind their quarry for the kill. But McConnell realized what they were doing: "This time I was sure it was a set up [but] they lost their timing and I jumped on the tail of one of them and really poured the fire to him [with his plane's .50-caliber machine guns]. Smoke came from his tail and I plowed right through it. The [enemy pilot] then pulled up, opened his speed brakes and bailed out."[72]

McConnell survived Korea only to be killed in 1954 while testing an experimental jet. But, like other fighter pilots of the Korean War, McConnell had helped pioneer a new era in aerial warfare—one that was seemingly more daring and deadly than any that had ever come before.

Winged Warfare

By the Korean War, military aviation had advanced greatly since World War I, when airplanes were used mainly to scout enemy positions, sometimes by taking photographs. However, aviation historian Jim Wilson writes that it was not long before pilots flying primitive aircraft like the Curtiss P-1 began engaging each other in combat, even though the primitive aircraft were constructed of wood and cloth, had double-decker sets of wings, open cockpits, and flew only 165 miles per hour:

> The passive use of aircraft as observation platforms changed rapidly in the opening weeks of World War I as rival pilots and their passengers began attacking each other. Fighters, which Americans insisted upon calling pursuit planes, were equipped with machine guns and [had] timing mechanisms to protect their propellers [the bullets had to pass through the propellers because the guns were mounted in front of the pilot].[73]

The first plane-to-plane battle, nicknamed a "dogfight," took place during World War I in October 1914 when a French plane shot down a German aircraft. A new style of combat had been born, and the war created flying legends such as American Eddie Rickenbacker and German Manfred von Richthofen, who is more famous as "the Red Baron."

Three decades later, in World War II, air power played a much bigger role. Improvements in engine performance, design, and construction enabled airplanes to fly faster, up to four hundred miles an hour, and travel hundreds of miles. Almost all were still driven by propellers and were powered by conventional engines.

The Germans, however, had developed a jet engine, a new way to power planes that made them fly faster and farther, and during the war it manufactured jet planes. The most famous was the Messerschmitt 262. Considered World War II's best fighter, it had a top speed of 540 miles per hour and a range 650 miles. But Germany was unable to produce many jets, and the planes did not play a significant role in the war. The United States also evolved this technology late in the war, but no U.S. jets made it into battle.

Thus, the Korean War was the first conflict in which jet airplanes met in combat. The inaugural jet-to-jet battle came on November 8, 1950, when a group of MiG-15s, a fighter jet developed by the Soviet Union, attacked U.S. Air Force (USAF) pilots flying F-80 Shooting Star jets. The F-80s were protecting B-29s that were going to bomb the Sinuiju airfield. During the encounter, Lt. Russell J. Brown shot down a MiG. The F-80s were effective combat planes in certain situations, but they were not the best U.S.

jet fighter. That title belonged to the newer, faster F-86.

U.S. Air Force F-80 Shooting Star fighters were involved in the world's first jet-to-jet battles in 1950 versus MiG-15s.

UN Fighter Jets

The premier United Nations fighter jet was the F-86, but none were available when the war began. The scarcity of F-86s mirrored America's initial lack of equipment and personnel to fight a ground war in Korea. Once again, this was due to the naive belief of the nation's military and political leaders that it would never again have to fight a conventional war. Explains historian Stanley Sandler, "The reason for the United States Air Force's lack of preparedness for the air war that soon developed in Korea was simple: that service saw its primary mission as basically the nuclear

bombing of Soviet industrial and political targets."[74]

The military thought F-86s were needed in Europe to protect bombers if they had to fly such missions. Suddenly, however, U.S. planes in Korea had to engage in jet fighter combat. At first the USAF had only the outmoded F-80, America's first mass-produced jet fighter. Initially designated the P-80, the plane's name was changed in 1948 to F-80 when *P* for "Pursuit" was changed to *F* for "Fighter." The F-80 had a wingspan of nearly thirty-nine feet, was thirty-four feet long, just over eleven feet tall, and weighed 16,856 pounds. The F-80 was armed with six .50-caliber machine guns and could carry 2,000 pounds of bombs. Its top speed was 580 miles per hour, and its cruising range, a distance limited by the gasoline it could carry, was 1,090 miles.

Although originally designed as a high-altitude fighter, in Korea the F-80 was mainly used for low-level rocket, bomb, and napalm attacks against ground targets instead of jet-to-jet combat. To many aviation historians, Brown's historic victory in that first-ever duel between jets was a near miracle. For one thing, five of his plane's six .50-caliber machine guns, his only weapons, were jammed. More important, the MiG-15—its designation was a combination of the last names of its Soviet design-ers, Mikoyan and Guryevich—was a better fighter than the F-80, an older model that was one hundred miles per hour slower and not as maneuverable.

UN officials soon realized they needed the F-86 Sabre, which was superior to the older jets, to counteract the speedy, lethal MiG. Although the F-86 had a shorter cruising range of only 835 miles, its top speed was 717 miles an hour. The F-86 had a wingspan of thirty-seven feet, was forty feet long, fifteen feet high, and weighed 12,470 pounds. The F-86 was armed with six .50-caliber machine guns that each fired five hundred bullets a minute.

The F-86's greater speed and maneuverability were due to a new wing design; wings were swept back at an angle of thirty-five degrees instead of sticking straight

The F-86: Fun to Fly

Air force colonel Walker "Bud" Mahurin was an ace in two different wars. During World War II Mahurin recorded 21 kills while flying a P-47, and during the Korean War he had 3.5 kills piloting an F-86 Sabre jet. Mahurin was shot down in both conflicts and became a prisoner of war in Korea. In "Bud Mahurin on the F-86," an interview on a website devoted to combat pilots, Mahurin explains how exhilarating it was to fly the plane:

> You had a sense of power, a sense of high performance. You didn't think much about the airplane. It felt like a part of you. In combat, you didn't think "I'm going to turn now, and I'm going to pull back on the stick." You just did it automatically, like moving an extension of your body. That was quite thrilling, and [flying it was] more fun than anything else I've ever done. The F-86 was a brilliant design. It was just a delight; it didn't have any bad habits. Unlike the MiG, creature comforts were taken into consideration. The Sabre had an air conditioning system that would produce ice if you wanted it to. It would drive you out of the cockpit with heat if you wanted. You could adjust it like a modern car. The MiG didn't have any of that. The MiG pilot was sitting in the cockpit without any air-conditioning. Our G-suits [flight suits] helped us control our blood flow at high maneuvering rates, and the Russians didn't have that either. There are more advantages—the F-86 was a Cadillac; the MiG-15 was a Model-T Ford.

out as they were on conventional aircraft and early jets like the F-80. This innovation grew out of research by German scientists that fell into the hands of U.S. and Soviet aircraft designers following World War II. Basically, the altered wing angle kept air from compressing in front of the aircraft at high speeds, something that slowed down planes and caused handling problems. Synonymous with Korean War fighter combat, the F-86 began operations there on December 15, 1950.

MiG-15

Until China entered the war in November 1950, Communist air power had been negligible—most of North Korea's planes were quickly destroyed in the opening weeks of the conflict, and those that remained were outclassed in the sky by superior UN planes. But China had the MiG-15, and it was a great fighter plane.

The MiG had a wingspan of thirty-three feet, was thirty-five feet long, just over twelve feet high, and weighed 8,115 pounds. With a swept-wing design similar to the F-86, it had a top speed of 670 miles per hour and a range of over 700 miles. The main difference was its armament. Instead of machine guns, the MiG had two 23 mm cannons and one 37 mm cannon. The cannons, which were mounted on the

A U.S. Air Force F-86 Sabre (at left) is chased by an enemy MiG-15 jet fighter during a high-speed dogfight.

front part of the plane, shot large explosive projectiles that could punch lethal holes in enemy aircraft. Air Force captain Harold Fischer, who flew an F-86 against MiGs, said he and his fellow pilots nicknamed the projectiles the cannons fired "golf balls." He admitted it was a strange experience to be the target of this weapon: "They [the cannon projectiles] had somewhat of the appearance of luminescent golf balls which grew into tennis balls as they passed the aircraft. You could become fascinated, almost hypnotized, by them. It was exhilaration to be shot at and missed."[75]

Just as the advent of Chinese infantry transformed the ground war, the arrival of MiGs dramatically altered aerial combat.

F-86 Sabre Versus MiG

The mechanical characteristics of the two planes were fairly equal, making the Sabre and the MiG worthy opponents. Although these two jet fighters were far superior to other planes of that era, each had its individual strengths and weaknesses. Armament was the biggest difference—machine guns versus cannons. An explanation on the website of the the U.S. Air Force Military Museum at Wright-Patterson Air Force Base claims that in the high-speed aerial combat the planes engaged in, machine guns were a better weapon than cannons:

The MiG fired heavier, more destructive shells at a slower rate while the Sabre's guns fired [heavy caliber ma-

An F-86 Team Makes a Kill

When they engaged MiG-15 planes in fighter combat, F-86 pilots worked closely in two-man teams. The two pilots not only attacked together but also helped protect one another in their deadly aerial duels high in the sky. In *No Bugles, No Drums: An Oral History of the Korean War*, edited by Rudy Tomedi, U.S. Air Force pilot Doug Carter explains how he and his partner, Ira Porter, fought with and shot down a MiG-15:

Ira got behind this MiG and the MiG pilot headed for the ground. He dropped from thirty thousand feet to probably two or three thousand. This guy was jinking [moving erratically] and turning and doing everything possible to get away. Ira had been firing at him for quite a while, and finally he fired out, ran out of ammunition. So I moved in behind the MiG. By this time we were in the mountains, and he was twisting down through the valleys and over the hills and going around mountains [and they were chasing him] like cops and robbers. I hit him with several good bursts and finally I caught him with a burst right behind the canopy [where the pilot sat]. He lit up like a Christmas tree. It looked like he lost control of his airplane. He was in a hard left turn and the next thing I knew he hit the side of a mountain and disintegrated. After he exploded, God, I was so damn excited. Seeing all that happen right in front of my eyes. It was like something you see in the movies.

chine gun bullets] at a much higher rate of fire. In high-speed dogfights typical of [the Korean War] Communist pilots found it very difficult to get hits on the F-86s they faced. On the other hand, Sabre pilots frequently only damaged MiGs because their machine guns lacked the punch of a cannon.[76]

The cannons were more effective against larger planes such as bombers, the original purpose for which they had been devised. However, pilots who fought MiGs, such as Doug Carter, who flew one hundred missions against the Soviet fighter after arriving in Korea in October 1952, had a fine appreciation for the lethal nature of MiG cannons: "You could say they had us outgunned. Six .50 caliber machine guns in the F-86 to three heavy nose cannons in the MiG. You looked over your shoulder and you saw this little puff . . . puff puff . . . that was about the rate of fire of that 37mm [cannon]. They had heavier guns."[77]

There were also differences in how the two planes flew. The F-86 was faster, and, because it was heavier, it could dive more quickly to lower altitudes. But the lighter MiG could outclimb the Sabre to all altitudes, an advantage it used in some of its dogfight tactics. "They'd dive at you," said Carter, "fire a burst, and then climb for altitude again, because the MiG-15 could climb faster."[78] The MiG could also climb higher than the F-86, which had a ceiling—the top altitude it could reach—of 45,600 feet compared to 51,000 for the MiG. That was a big tactical advantage because it meant that a MiG could climb high enough to escape a pursuing F-86.

However, Air Force colonel Walker "Bud" Mahurin, who had 3.5 MiG kills, points out that the F-86 also had a major advantage because of the location of the aircraft's horizontal stabilizer. The F-86's horizontal stabilizer—a piece of metal angled a certain way that enabled the plane to handle better—was mounted lower than that of the MiG stabilizer. Mahurin said this placement decreased the Soviet plane's maneuverability:

When the MiG-15 got into a spin, the air flying off the main wings would blanket out the horizontal stabilizer and the pilot couldn't recover. They [MiG pilots] were ordered to bail out if they got into a flat spin. The low stabilizer on the F-86 meant that we could outperform the MiG-15s in various combat maneuvers, especially turns, and so it offered an advantage over the MiG-15.[79]

The Korean War marked the public debut of the MiG-15, and debate still swirls today about whether the F-86 or the MiG-15 was the better fighter plane. However, Kum-Sok No, a North Korean pilot who defected on September 21, 1953, by flying his MiG to the Kimpo air base near Seoul, South Korea, votes for the F-86. Claimed No, "The MiG-15 was good, but hardly the superfighter that should strike terror in the heart of the West. There was no question that the F-86 was the better fighter."[80]

UN Combat Superiority

Based on their flight capabilities, the F-86 and the MiG-15 seemed equipped to fight

The MiG Pilot Who Defected

The guns of many MiG-15s during the Korean War bore the phrase "Pour out and zero in this vindictive ammunition to the damn Yankees [Americans]." This fact became known on September 23, 1953, when twenty-one-year-old Senior Lt. Kum-Sok No of the North Korean air force unexpectedly flew his MiG-15 into the Kimpo air base near Seoul. No claimed he was "sick and tired of the red [Communist] deceit." No was too late to collect a reward of one hundred thousand dollars that U.S. officials had posted for a MiG delivered intact—the truce that ended the war had gone into effect on July 27. However, U.S. officials were elated to get the plane. The explanation of what happened next to the plane comes from "The Story of the MiG-15 on Display," an article on the U.S. Air Force Museum website:

> The MiG-15 was taken to Okinawa [Japan] where it was first flown by Wright Field Test Pilot, Capt. H.E. "Tom" Collins. Subsequent test flights were made by Capt. Collins and

Maj. C.E. "Chuck" Yeager. The airplane was next disassembled and airlifted to Wright-Patterson AFB [Air Force Base] in Dec. 1953 where it was reassembled and given exhaustive flight-testing. The U.S. then offered to return the MiG to its rightful owners but when no country claimed the plane, it was transferred to the USAF Museum in 1957.

The plane is still on display at the base's museum. As for No, the Wright-Patterson Air Force Base website details what happened to the young pilot:

> Shortly after landing at Kimpo AB, the young pilot not only learned that his mother had been safely evacuated from North to South Korea in 1951 and that she was still alive and well. At his request, No came to the States, changed his name, and became a U.S. citizen. He graduated from the University of Delaware, he was joined by his mother, and he was married.

on nearly equal terms. But on December 17, 1950, Lt. Col. Bruce H. Hinton, commanding officer of the 336th Fighter-Interceptor Squadron, damaged one enemy plane and shot down another in the first Sabre-versus-MiG aerial confrontation. Hinton's victory set a pattern of domination that continued until the fighting ended.

During the Korean War, UN pilots—almost all of them were U.S. airmen—shot down 792 MiGs while losing only 76 Sabres, a victory ratio of more than ten to one. Carter says the reason for this combat superiority was simple: "Pilot for pilot, we had them beat hands down."[81] Carter's

comment could be dismissed as the boast of a biased participant. But in *The Korean War*, author Max Hastings, a historian from England, comes to the same conclusion: "The American pilots were of higher quality than the [Communists]."[82]

The main reason UN pilots excelled is that aerial combat is a specialized, complex type of flying, and many of them had valuable experience from their battles in World War II. Even though the jets they now flew were much faster and had different, though far superior, handling qualities, their experience gave them an edge over the Chinese and North Korean pilots

The Face of the Enemy

Air force colonel Harold Fischer was a "double ace"—he shot down ten enemy aircraft, twice the number needed to achieve the distinction of being designated an ace. It was when Fischer shot down his fifth plane, a MiG-15, that the cruel nature of his job was emotionally imprinted on his mind. His experience in that action is from *Hotshots: An Oral History of the Air Force Combat Pilots of the Korean War*, edited by Jennie Ethell Chancey and William R. Forstchen:

My fifth kill came sooner than I expected and with it a great deal of trepidation and mental anguish. [After hitting a MiG-15 with machine guns] I pulled up alongside to look at it. I wish I had not. The pilot was beating on the canopy, trying to escape. The heat must have been insufferable, since the canopy was changing color and the

smoke was intense. Up to that moment, the enemy had been impersonal—each aircraft a target that had little meaning and not associated with flesh and blood. But the sight of another man trapped in the cockpit of a burning aircraft with no power and no place to land was a psychological fact impossible for me to forget. Seeing me, the pilot attempted to turn his aircraft and evidently ram me. It was easy for me to evade him by moving out to the side. There was only one thing for me to do: to put the pilot out of his misery as quickly as possible. Sliding behind the MiG, the molten metal of his airplane came over mine like a light rain shower and partially obscured my windshield. I pulled up the nose to fire and squeezed off a few short rounds.

Soviet-designed MiG-15 jet fighters (pictured) were evenly matched against U.S. F-86 Sabres in air combat.

they faced. In *Hotshots*, their book about jet fighter pilots, Jennie Ethell Chancey and William R. Forstchen explain how lack of experience handicapped Communist pilots: "Regarding the Chinese and North Korean pilots it was generally acknowledged that they came into combat with a fairly good level of training, at times even superior training. But as a whole they lacked the imaginative skills [veteran pilots had learned in combat]."[83]

However, Chancey and Forstchen explain that some MiG-15s were piloted by superior fliers who often won aerial battles:

"[There were] a certain few who clearly stood out on the other side. An enemy who broke the mold and who seemed to be one step ahead of us was an anomaly. These anomalies gave our pilots the ultimate challenge . . . creating speculation as to their identity."[84]

Soviet Pilots in Korea

Many of those "anomalies" were actually Soviet pilots, a fact that was not made public until many years later (even though U.S. officials knew during the war that Soviets were flying in Korea). Their World War II combat experience was as great as the Americans', which enabled them to fight better. Air force captain Bill Lilley remembers the shock of seeing a Soviet pilot's face after he bailed out of a MiG that Lilley shot down: "[He] passed immediately over my canopy, inches from my head. The pilot [was] still in the [ejected] seat, upside down . . . a shock of blond hair and a wildly contorted face were instantly burned into my memory. I can still see that face today. I was queried many times about the pilot's shock of blond hair—very unusual but true."[85]

Lilley and other pilots were interviewed in detail about such sightings because UN officials suspected that Soviet pilots were flying; the truth did not come out until the 1990s, when Communist military records explaining what had occurred were released. Soviet pilots were ordered to try to conceal their identities during combat. Dmitri Samoilov, who was credited with

shooting down ten UN planes in Korea, explains how ridiculous the effort was: "In the middle of an attack, I was supposed to figure out how to say something in Chinese. Of course, we used Russian. And of course, we knew everyone could hear [our Soviet radio communications]."[86]

Samoilov, however, understood why he and other pilots were ordered to disguise their identities. "If we had fought openly," he admits, "it probably would have come to nuclear weapons. And who wanted that? Americans? Russians? It would have been terrible."[87] The fear that the war could spread to directly involve the United States and the Soviet Union, possibly leading to nuclear war, was also the reason that UN officials never made an issue of the fact that Soviet pilots flew in Korea.

MiG Alley

The arrival of MiG-15s, no matter who was piloting them, changed the way in which UN forces conducted their massive bombing campaign. The MiGs attacked bombers so successfully—in one week in late 1951 they shot down five B-29 Superfortresses—that UN bombers began attacking only at night, when they were safer from attack.

The F-86s tried to protect bombers on their missions, but there were too few of them to do the job. Although only a handful of MiG-15s began combat in Korea, by the end of the conflict there were more than 900 of them. This contrasted sharply with the fact that the U.S. Air Force never had more than about 150 F-86s in

Korea, and often as many as half of them were out of commission due to a shortage of parts. It was only the superior flying skills of UN pilots that helped overcome the huge numerical advantage the Communists enjoyed in jet fighters.

The main task for the F-86 was to keep MiG-15 jet fighters busy so they could not attack UN forces farther south. To do this, the F-86s went hunting daily for enemy fighters in what became known as MiG Alley, a narrow triangle of land south of the Yalu River in the northwestern corner of Korea. They would fly the alley in long figure eights, hoping to intercept enemy planes.

MiGs operated there freely from airfields just north of the Yalu in China, where they were safe from attack. UN officials left the bases alone because they feared that if they struck China directly, the war could further escalate. UN planes were also not allowed to cross the border into China to fight MiGs unless they were in what was called "hot pursuit" during a dogfight. Air force colonel Walker "Bud" Mahurin admits that the restrictions bothered pilots:

> The rules of combat prohibited us from crossing into Manchuria [a Chinese province], across the Yalu River. The State Department didn't want us

Despite being severely outnumbered by enemy MiG-15s, U.S. F-86 pilots (pictured) used superior flying skills to control Korean skies.

flying over China, and possibly provoking them to escalate the war in Korea. As we flew above the Yalu, we could see the MiG-15s taking off from their sanctuaries, climbing up above our altitude, then diving down to build up speed, and coming across to do combat with us. We were like a prize fighter fighting with one arm tied behind his back.[88]

Aerial Combat

Even with that restriction, UN pilots had no trouble finding enemy planes to battle. Operating from the Kimpo air base near Seoul, the F-86s would fly two hundred miles north to MiG Alley seeking opponents. Air force captain Bill Lilley explains that in such combat situations, the Sabres operated in units of four planes:

Our basic fighting unit was a flight of four aircraft in fingertip formation. Large gaggles [groups of planes] had been tried in the first engagements between MiGs and Sabres and had been found to be unnecessary. They were too cumbersome and reduced flexibility. Under attack the four-ship flight would often break down into two elements of two aircraft each, the lead aircraft firing, the wingman clearing [protecting the other plane]. The wingman was our unsung hero. This was tough duty that required the utmost in flying skill and discipline.[89]

John Glenn was an ace fighter pilot in Korea, and became a famous astronaut after the war.

During combat engagements, at least two pilots always worked together. If a leader and his wingman became separated or if one of their planes malfunctioned or was damaged so that it could not fly, they were to return to base because it was too dangerous for a lone plane to fight the enemy. In July 1953 John Glenn, a U.S. Marine Corps pilot who downed three MiGs but later became more famous as an astronaut and U.S. senator, found out how dangerous this situation could be.

Glenn's wingman, Jerry Parker, was hit after their flight of four F-86s was attacked by sixteen MiGs. When Glenn broke off to escort Parker back to Kimpo, six MiGs pursued them. Glenn's only hope was to attack the superior force himself, which he did. His boldness forced the half-dozen planes to break off the attack, but Glenn chased them and shot down one plane. Even Glenn was amazed he survived the encounter: "The MiGs' tactics were so poor I could only imagine it was a training flight, or they were low on fuel, but we were unbelievably lucky."[90]

Gaining Experience

The Korean War changed fighter plane combat forever. In the future, only jet aircraft would be used for this dramatic form of fighting. This was something both the United States and the Soviet Union, the two main Cold War foes, realized right away; and they took advantage of the conflict to sharpen those skills for future wars. Historian Max Hastings claims, "The Soviets, like America [and its allies], used Korea as a proving ground where their pilots could be rotated in and out, to gain experience of the new shape of air warfare."[91]

Chapter 6

Psychological Warfare: Words as Weapons

Rifles, hand grenades, jet planes, tanks, and artillery pieces were not the only weapons used to fight the Korean War. United Nations and Communist forces who battled physically in the air, on the sea, and on the ground also used words to weaken each other, to influence world opinion, and to convince enemy soldiers to quit fighting and join their side.

This strange war of words began the day North Korea invaded South Korea. On June 25, 1950, North Korean leader Kim Il Sung declared to the world that his country had been forced to fight because of South Korea's rejection of "all methods for peaceful reunification proposed by the Democratic People's Republic of Korea [North Korea]." He even claimed that the nation his army had invaded, on his own orders, had been the first to commit "armed aggression north of the 38th parallel."[92] Kim's statement was meant to be a political justification of his nation's sur-

prise attack. The only problem was that Kim was lying; it was his country that began the war.

The United States also employed words to twist the truth into its own version of reality. When President Harry S. Truman was asked at a news conference on June 29 to characterize the fighting in Korea, he had a strange response: "We are not at war. The members of the United Nations [UN] are going to the relief of the Korean [people] to suppress a bandit raid on the Republic of Korea."[93] When a reporter pressed Truman whether the fighting was a "police action" rather than a "war," the president responded, "Yes, that is exactly what it amounts to."[94]

Although it is hard to believe that any armed conflict that would last three years and take the lives of 36,940 U.S. soldiers was a police action and not a full-scale war, it suited Truman's purposes to label it that. Truman believed the phrase downgraded the seriousness of the conflict, making it less likely other Communist nations would join the fighting and expand it into another world war. He also believed it put the situation in terms of good versus evil—the good UN "policemen," led by the United States, were trying to stop the bad "bandit" North Koreans, who had illegally attacked their neighbor.

The Korean War was a much more complicated situation than the two leaders made it out to be with such simplistic, distorted statements. But those comments were only two uses of propaganda, which was part of one of the war's most potent weapons—psychological warfare.

Harry S. Truman served as commander in chief of America's armed forces throughout much of the Korean War.

Propaganda and Psychological Warfare

The *Encyclopaedia Brittanica* defines propaganda as the "dissemination of reformation—facts, arguments, rumors, half-truths, or lies—to influence public opinion."[95] Propaganda is the main weapon in psychological warfare, a type of combat as distinct as aerial or naval battle. Stephen E. Pease defines propaganda in his book on psychological warfare in the Korean War:

> Psychological warfare is the attempt by one nation to gain an advantage over another by exploiting fear, mistrust, suspicion, rumor, prejudice, and what [German military strategist Carl] von Clausewitz identified as an often decisive principle of war, uncertainty, to influence international opinion and/or the frame of mind of opposing soldiers. The goal is to affect the enemy's mind and persuade him to take an action, even against his conscious will, that is favorable to his opponent.[96]

Psychological warfare had been used in many other previous wars. It was employed even more in Korea because that conflict was part of the broader Cold War between the United States and the Soviet Union. Propaganda was one of the main weapons in the Cold War, the battle for world domination between the political philosophies of democracy and communism. Thus, it was no surprise that the two sides used it during the Korean War, the Cold War's first armed conflict.

Reeducating American POWs

When Communists assumed power in a country like North Korea, they created reeducation programs that required people, sometimes forcibly, to learn and adopt their political philosophy. During the Korean War, they did the same thing to prisoners of war. Nick Tosques, who served in the army's 555th Field Artillery Battalion, was captured on April 25, 1951; he spent two and a half years in a North Korean prison camp. In *No Bugles, No Drums: An Oral History of the Korean War*, edited by Rudy Tomedi, Tosques explains what reeducation was like:

> We were given lectures every day. "You're capitalist. Your government lies to you. The rich people don't care about you, that's why they sent you over here to die. Your government makes war to oppress the Korean people." That kind of baloney. We had to learn about communism. The only way to live. The only way to go. How under communism everyone is equal. We had to listen to that stuff every single day. The mornings were for hard labor. The afternoon was study time. We'd study about how capitalism was no good. How the working man was exploited. How communism was the only way to go. And we had guys who turned, who fell for that baloney. Not right away but it was pounded and pounded and pounded into us. Every day. Every day. Capitalism no, communism yes. Like most of the others, I went along with it: "Yeah, yeah, yeah. You're right. You're right." But in the back of our minds all we're thinking about is home. About getting out, getting back, going to work. You couldn't completely ignore the lessons, because in the mass study session they would ask you what you learned. What are you studying? Do you know how your government lies to you? That your [President] Harry Truman lies. That he will never get you home.

A Leaflet War

UN and Communist forces waged an intense propaganda campaign to demoralize enemy soldiers and scare them into surrendering. One of the most common forms this effort took was printed material. Using leaflets, each side tried to convince opposing soldiers that their side was morally or politically wrong, that they did not have a chance to win, and that they would be killed.

On June 31, 1950, less than a day after Truman committed U.S. soldiers to Korea, planes flew over the battle zone and dropped the first UN-printed propaganda. In the war's largest propaganda drop, the 12 million leaflets prepared by the U.S. military's Psychological Warfare Section promised South Korean soldiers and civilians that the UN would save them from the Communists. Later in the war, leaflets were used to scare enemy soldiers. One released prior to a battle had this dire warning from Gen. Matthew B. Ridgway, who commanded the Eighth Army:

> Comrades! Soldiers of the North Korean Army. U.N. airplanes are overhead prepared to strike your positions. They are loaded with rockets, napalm and [explosives]. U.N. artillery is sighting on you. At my command they will

bring you death. You have seen your positions littered with the burned, blackened, and shattered bodies of your buddies after our planes and artillery come down upon you. Raise both hands high over your head and walk in the open toward U.N. lines. You are guaranteed good treatment. Act now. You have five minutes.[97]

During the war, UN forces showered more than 2.5 billion leaflets on Communist soldiers. Many leaflets on both sides were in the form of safe-conduct surrender passes guaranteeing combatants that they would be welcomed by the soldiers they were fighting; interviews with prisoners indicated their greatest fear in surrendering was that they would be killed. Historian Stanley Sandler states that UN officials stated that "about one-third [of Communists] claimed to have surrendered in part because of psychological warfare leaflets. Nearly every prisoner voluntarily taken had one or more leaflets."[98]

Ranging in size from three inches by five inches to that of a newspaper, UN leaflets were dropped from planes—B-29 crews called such missions paper routes, as if they were delivering newspapers—and via special artillery shells that exploded harmlessly and spread them over a wide area. A B-29 could drop 1 million leaflets each night.

Although a few Communist leaflets were tossed out of small planes by "Bedcheck Charlies" during their nighttime

Safe conduct passes dropped by UN planes guaranteed honorable treatment for Communist soldiers willing to surrender.

flights, UN air superiority made Communists rely on artillery shells to send propaganda. Sometimes, their soldiers delivered leaflets in person, sneaking into UN areas and scattering them by hand. Communist messages sought to manipulate the feelings of loneliness and homesickness that UN soldiers had. Communist leaflets were often grammatically incorrect and poorly worded. The following excerpt is from one titled "Your Folks at Home Need You":

Your dear mother is filling with tears in her eyes. Your pretty and young wife is going to crazy, for she can't stand any longer. Your children are crying and asking where their daddy is now. American officers and soldiers; Do you like to leave your mother, wife and children for the cannon fodders of Truman and [Gen. Douglas] MacArthur? Just cease fighting and come over to our line. We guarantee you safe conduct, warm clothes, good food and medical care if you injure, and in the end you'll get home.[99]

Communist soldiers also scrawled propaganda on walls in villages when they retreated. In November 1950 advancing UN soldiers saw this message: "American officers and soldiers: 5000 miles from home, fighting 30000000 Koreams and behind them are 475000000 Chinses. What can bombs do? They canont kill all our people, They can only stiffen our fighting spirit."[100]

Verbal Propaganda

Written propaganda, however, was not the only way the two sides tried to demoralize each other. The day after the first leaflets rained down on combatants, UN radio began broadcasting messages of hope to South Korean soldiers and civilians. For the rest of the war, Voice of the UN Command and Voice of America broadcasts to China and both Koreas contained updated news on the war and propaganda aimed at soldiers and civilians.

In the radio war, both sides made allegations that their opponents were motivated by ulterior motives for fighting—the UN wanted to profit from Korea's land and other resources, the Communists wanted to conquer more territory—and accusations of cruelty and war atrocities. To get UN soldiers to listen, the Communists mixed popular music with propaganda messages on shows beamed from Pyongyang, North Korea, hosted by "Seoul City Sue," an English-speaking announcer. U.S. soldiers, however, enjoyed the music on such shows while ignoring the propaganda messages.

When the fighting became stabilized along a static front during the last two years of the conflict, a loudspeaker war began. Both sides blared messages that tried to scare enemy soldiers and make them less effective fighters. Communist loudspeakers focused on the theme of homesickness by playing American music that made soldiers dream of being with their loved ones. On Christmas Eve, the Communists even tried to play "Jingle Bells" and "Silent Night" on the bugles they used to communicate with during battle.

Because of its superiority in equipment, the UN had two additional methods of using loudspeakers—by mounting them on airplanes and tanks. C-47 cargo planes with loudspeakers would fly over

Communist Leaflets

Leaflets were a major weapon that Communists used against UN soldiers. In an article in the *Falling Leaf* magazine, P.H. Robbs states that the North Koreans and Chinese "attached great importance to every form of propaganda and . . . used this weapon most effectively." Some leaflets they distributed had facsimile signatures of captured American soldiers and a message they supposedly wrote to their "G.I. [infantry] Buddies," such as the following: "Have you ever stopped to think what you are fighting for? Stop! Just stop! And think it over. I say we shouldn't be fighting these people. I say we have no reason to fight, no reason to fight these people whatsoever! We are fighting the people who are fighting for the freedom of their country. This is their country and not ours. We should withdraw from Korea."

Another leaflet Robbs quotes tried to ease fears UN soldiers had about how Communists treated prisoners so that they would be more willing to give up:

I am a prisoner of war under the care of the People's Army. I make an appeal to you.

Stop this useless fighting and lay down your arms as I did. Don't believe what you were told about being killed or tortured! You will be treated kindly. I have been well-fed and housed since the first day of my capture. I, too, was afraid to surrender, but believe me, buddy, it is the best bet. Use your head! Don't die on foreign soil for nothing.

Some leaflets were in the form of surrender passes, such as this one Robbs cites:

ORDER. The Bearer, regardless of his nationality or rank, will be duly accepted and escorted to a rear People's Volunteer Garrison or POW Camp, and on arrival will be guaranteed in accordance with our policy of leniency to prisoners of war the following four great affirmations:

1. Security of life
2. Retention of all personal belongings
3. Freedom from maltreatment or abuse
4. Medical care for the wounded
THE CHINESE PEOPLE'S VOLUNTEERS' HEADQUARTERS

UN soldiers examine the contents of a Communist propaganda bomb found in North Korea (below left), and read a message urging American troops to surrender and leave.

the enemy to broadcast propaganda. Historian Edgar O'Ballance explains that this "had the advantage that the message got through to all within earshot, and there was nothing the Communists could do to prevent this, except improve air defenses and hustle their men underground."[101] The Communists tried to stop other UN propaganda by punishing soldiers found with leaflets and making noise to drown out ground-level loudspeakers.

The flights, however, were dangerous; low-flying planes were easy targets and almost always returned to their base with bullet holes. Another hazard were cables that Communists strung across narrow valleys to snare low-flying aircraft. A safer alternative was "talking tanks," which drove past the enemy while playing messages such as, "We are always ready to greet you with torrents of fire. Cease fighting now and save your life for your family."[102] The soldiers were relatively safe, but the vibration and noise from the rumbling tanks often distorted the sound.

International Warfare

Psychological warfare was not confined to the battlefield. Because the Korean War was an extension of the Cold War between the United States and the Soviet Union and their allies, both sides waged a worldwide propaganda war concerning the events unfolding in Korea. The object of this campaign was to win the support of other nations and to weaken the resolve of their opponent to keep fighting. This part of the conflict was fought through statements by officials, stories in the news media, and diplomatic maneuvering.

For example, on June 27, 1950, Truman told the American people that North Korea's attack on South Korea showed that "communism has passed beyond the use of subversion to conquer independent nations and will now use armed invasion and war."[103] Like most people at the time, Truman believed that the Soviet Union had ordered North Korea to attack South Korea. Although it was learned decades later that North Korea decided on its own to begin fighting, Truman's comment succeeded in making other countries fear that the Soviet Union might initiate similar attacks on them.

In order to make the conflict seem less a battle strictly between the United States and communism, Truman had also wisely gotten the United Nations, which he helped organize in 1945, to head the effort to save South Korea. But although the resolution the UN Security Council adopted on June 27 made that new peace organization the authorizing power in Korea, the United States and South Korea contributed 90 percent of the manpower, and it was the United States, not the UN, that provided the weapons and equipment to fight there.

Soviet leaders like Joseph Stalin also used the war for their own purposes. Stalin, who believed the conflict would weaken the U.S. military by tying it up in Asia, was in no hurry to end the fighting once it

Using loudspeakers to spread propaganda in the battlefield became a common practice for both sides during the war's final two years.

began. When peace talks started on July 10, 1951, Stalin messaged Chinese leader Mao Tse-tung, who headed the Communist side, to proceed slowly in reaching an agreement. Stalin believed that American citizens, who were becoming dismayed by the large numbers of U.S. soldiers being killed, would start exerting pressure on their leaders to end the fighting: "This war," he boasted, "is getting on America's nerves."[104] Stalin thought that dragging out peace talks would increase chances that UN forces could give up or, at the very least, offer better terms to end the fighting.

In May 1952, when Maj. Gen. William K. Harrison assumed command of the UN negotiating team, Harrison showed that he understood the Soviet ploy. Harrison characterized Communist stall tactics during peace negotiations as "fighting with words and not with guns, just trying to prevent us from getting an armistice which we wanted. And so we would give up and go home."[105]

Charges of Biological Warfare

This global propaganda war included accusations by both sides that their opponents committed atrocities such as killing civilians and murdering soldiers after they surrendered. Although both sides were guilty of some brutal acts, most allegations were either false or grossly distorted to make them seem much worse.

One of the most effective charges was that the United States engaged in biological warfare. On March 26, 1952, Chinese premier Chou En-lai wrote the United Nations to claim the United States had spread smallpox, cholera, and other diseases in China by dropping bombs and shooting artillery shells containing beetles, lice, ticks, and other insects infected with deadly germs. Chou accused America of "invading China and threatening the security of the Chinese people by the criminal and vicious device of mass slaughter of peaceful people."[106]

By 1950 the United States, the Soviet Union, and some other countries had developed biological warfare programs. However, on June 20, 1950, the National Security Council, a panel that advises the president, had issued a document that reaffirmed the U.S. policy of never using biological weapons unless another nation used them first.

When the charge was repeated by Soviet leaders, President Truman vehemently denied the accusation: "The Kremlin [Soviet Union leaders] cries that we have used germ warfare. There isn't a word of truth in that. We have never [done something like that] in our operations in Korea. And they know that. They know it well."[107] Documents made public since the war ended show that Soviet leaders

knew the charge was a hoax but kept repeating it to embarrass America and pressure it to end the conflict.

This allegation has been researched and investigated thoroughly by historians, and the consensus is that it was false. Propaganda, however, does not have to be

Chinese premier Chou En-lai claimed the United States used biological warfare to spread disease.

true to be effective. Historian O'Ballance writes, "The success of this Communist propaganda was so great that even [decades after the war ended], despite ample evidence to the contrary, many who are not Communists firmly believe that germ warfare was waged by the Americans in the Korean War."[108] A main reason some countries believed the charge was that nineteen captured U.S. airmen admitted they took part in such aerial attacks. Their dramatic written and recorded statements made the allegation seem true. After the war, however, they all said they had made the statements because their captors threatened to torture or kill them. This manipulation of UN prisoners of war (POWs) was only one example of the most brutal part of the psychological warfare waged in Korea—the use of this form of combat on captured soldiers.

UN Prisoners of War

The Geneva Convention, which was ratified by most nations on August 12, 1949, contains a strict, legalistic description concerning how soldiers captured in battle must be treated. The convention stipulates that "persons taking no active part in the hostilities, including members of armed forces who have laid down their arms and those placed hors de combat [unable to fight] by sickness, wounds, detention, or any other cause, shall in all circumstances be treated humanely."[109]

Although psychological warfare usually attacks people's minds rather than their bodies, its techniques can include brutal physical assaults. The best example of this is the barbaric way in which North Korean and Chinese captors tortured UN POWs to make them switch allegiance and support communism. During the Korean War, the Communists openly ignored this international treaty. They subjected UN POWs to inhumane, brutal living conditions in prison camps, tortured them for information, and subjected them to reeducation programs designed to make them believe in communism. U.S. soldiers were treated especially harshly; of the 7,140 Americans who were captured, 2,701 died in captivity.

The Communists forced defenseless prisoners to contribute to the Communist psychological warfare effort by making statements that hurt their country. Some of the messages were relatively harmless, as in the recordings Radio Peking broadcast in which American and British captives claimed, or seemed to indicate, that the Communists were treating them well. This is part of a statement by one U.S. soldier: "Hello, this is Marine Andrew Condron speaking. Hello, Mum, Dad, and all at home. By courtesy of the Chinese People's 'Volunteers,' I am broadcasting to you now to tell you we are getting on here, and about our preparations for Christmas."[110]

Although many statements seemed harmless to the men who wrote or spoke them, the Communists benefited by appearing humane even though they generally treated POWs barbarically from the time they were captured. Historian Stanley Sandler describes how North Korean and Chinese prison guards handled Americans:

[North Koreans] seemed to take particularly brutal vengeance upon the "American imperialists." . . . U.S. POWs, usually survivors of a number of "death marches" [between prison camps], were paraded through the streets of Pyongyang. Their haggard, emaciated forms were frequently photographed and those photographs were given global distribution. Thus the North Koreans documented

their own barbarism. Those who survived the death marches and the shootings found themselves in camps in the far North with a continued ordeal of beatings, near-starvation and unrelenting physical and mental pressure to turn "progressive" and broadcast or write messages back home denouncing American "aggression" in Korea.[111]

The most damaging statements POWs were coerced into making were the "confessions" by airmen that they engaged in

UN prisoners of war were often subjected to inhumane living conditions and torture by their Communist captors.

Mimicking an Atomic Bomb Attack

Although the United States did not employ the atomic bomb during the Korean War, the threat of having the world's most destructive weapon used against them was one of the worst fears Communists could conceive. In *Korea: The Unknown War*, authors Jon Halliday and Bruce Cumings detail how the U.S. Air Force conducted bombing runs that mimicked dropping an atomic bomb. Their intent was to scare the enemy:

> In September and October 1951, while the peace talks were suspended over violations of the neutral zone and during the fiercest land battle of the war between US and North Korean troops, on Heartbreak Ridge, the US carried out "Operation Hudson Harbor" in conditions of utmost secrecy. Lone B-29 bombers flew over North Korea on simulated atomic-bombing runs, dropping dummy atomic bombs or heavy TNT bombs. The project called for "actual functioning of all activities which would be involved in an atomic strike, including weapons assembly and testing, leading ground control of the bomb aiming" and the like. Although the project indicated the bombs were probably not useful (for purely tactical reasons), one may imagine the steel nerves required of leaders in Pyongyang, observing on radar a lone B-29 [instead of large group of planes, which was their normal bombing formation] simulating the attack lines that had resulted in the devastation of Hiroshima and Nagasaki just six years earlier, each time unsure whether the bomb was real or a dummy.

biological warfare. Lt. John Quinn, for example, stated, "I was forced to be a tool of these warmongers, made to drop germ bombs, and do this awful crime."[112] However, the use of Communist rhetoric and the stilted, ungrammatical text of the statements indicated the prisoners were reading prepared scripts, leading many to realize that the POWs had been coerced into making them.

Brainwashing

The Communist mistreatment of prisoners extended far beyond forcing them to contribute to the psychological war being waged against their own forces. Historian Max Hastings states that the Korean War also "became notorious as the first modern conflict in which a combatant made a systematic attempt to convert prisoners to his own ideology."[113]

UN soldiers in North Korean and Chinese POW camps were subjected to daily doses of propaganda designed to make them believe communism was superior to the political and economic systems of their own nations. This effort became popularly known as brainwashing. Historian Edgar O'Ballance explains what this meant:

> [It] achieved notoriety as "brain washing," a phrase probably evolved from the colloquial Chinese "Hsi Nao," which literally means "to wash brain." The Communists called it "thought reform." The process consisted of lec-

tures and continuous, monotonous, single-minded repetition. The object was first of all to destroy existing beliefs and ideals and then to implant others in their place.[114]

A North Korean soldier taken as a prisoner of war awaits his escort to a UN POW camp.

The goal of thought reform, a process Communists also used on civilians in countries or areas they seized to make them easier to control, was to make POWs willing subjects in psychological war and to embarrass UN countries by having their soldiers turn Communist. When the war ended and POWs were released, slightly more than 300 UN soldiers defected to the enemy—21 Americans, 1 British soldier, and 325 South Koreans.

That was a relatively insignificant number, however, compared to the 21,809 Communist POWs, out of a total of 75,823 UN prisoners, who chose democracy by refusing to go home. Many North Koreans and Chinese defected despite an unprecedented Communist effort to avoid such an embarrassment by extending psychological warfare to UN prison camps.

Communist POWs

The issue that held up a cease-fire agreement to end the fighting for over a year was repatriation of prisoners. Truman and other UN leaders believed POWs should have the right to refuse to be repatriated—returned to their homelands—but the Communists demanded everyone be sent back. One reason they did this was because many Communist soldiers were not "volunteers," as had been previously claimed, but Chinese and Koreans who had been forced to fight and did not believe in communism. The Communists feared that these unwilling soldiers would use their capture as an opportunity to escape communism, which would embarrass China and North Korea.

The Communists therefore ordered trained agents to be captured so they could work inside UN camps to keep soldiers loyal. They were also instructed to incite violent disturbances that would make UN forces look bad after they were reported by the news media. These agents and other hard-line Communist prisoners also attacked POWs who wanted to defect.

However, Communist violence was only part of the brutality occurring in the camps. When UN officials began screening prisoners to see which ones wanted to be repatriated, South Korean prison guards—who often brutally treated their captives—and groups of anti-Communist prisoners retaliated against loyal Communists. Historians Jon Halliday and Bruce Cumings describe what happened: "The USA's first chief negotiator at the peace talks, Admiral [Turner] Joy, [wrote that] anyone who expressed a wish to return home was 'either beaten black and blue or killed [by anti-Communists] . . . the majority of the POWs were too terrified to frankly express their choice."[115]

A Powerful Weapon

The attempt to continue using psychological warfare against soldiers after they had been captured indicates the extent to which this form of combat was used during the Korean War. U.S. secretary of the army Frank Pace Jr. was a big believer in it, partly because he considered it the "cheapest form of warfare."[116] And even before the war began, the Communists were considered masters of psychological warfare because they had used it extensively to win control of Russia, China, and other nations.

In *Psywar*, Stephen E. Pease states that although psychological warfare was only a small part of the Korean War, it was a powerful and devastating weapon. Pease claims that the biggest lesson learned from the war about this form of combat was that "we were very unprepared for an enemy that would take our sons and daughters and use them against us so easily."[117]

The Weapon the United States Dared Not Use

At a news conference on November 30, 1950, President Harry S. Truman made a comment that sent a shock wave of fear hurtling around the world. He said, simply, that the United States was willing to use any weapon it had to win the Korean War, including the atomic bomb. "We will take whatever steps are necessary to meet the military situation, just as we always have,"[118] said Truman. When reporters pressed him about whether America was actually preparing to employ the dreaded weapon, Truman responded, "There has always been active consideration of its use. I don't want to see it used. It is a terrible weapon, and it should not be used on innocent, men, women and children who have nothing to do with this military aggression. That happens when it's used."[119] Truman's offhand remarks about possible use of the atomic bomb resulted the next day in front-page stories in newspapers around the world. And those news articles, even

though they contained only the mere mention that this terrible weapon might be unleashed, frightened tens of millions of people.

Fear of Nuclear War

The world's greatest fear in the 1950s was a nuclear war between the Cold War's main participants, the United States and the Soviet Union. Truman's remark about using the atomic bomb in Korea to help win the war scared people because they feared that the Soviets, who were backing North Korea, might respond with their own nuclear weapons if he did.

In 1950 the atomic bomb was a strange, new, and fearsome weapon. People had been awed and frightened by the devastation atomic bombs caused in August 1945 when the United States dropped them on Hiroshima and Nagasaki, killing more than one hundred thousand people and reducing the two Japanese cities to rubble. When the Soviet Union developed its own bomb

in 1949, people in many countries began to worry that nuclear war could destroy the world by spreading radiation around the globe.

Many people believed that the only thing worse than one nation having the atomic bomb was that two countries would be able to wield it in time of war. Even noted physicist Albert Einstein, who had helped America develop the world's first atomic bomb, claimed, "On both sides the means to mass destruction are perfected with feverish haste. In the end, there beckons more and more clearly general annihilation."[120]

Suggested but Not Used

Despite Truman's comments in his frightening news conference, the United States

An atomic bomb was dropped on Hiroshima, Japan, to end World War II, but weapons of mass destruction were not necessary in Korea.

never came close to employing the atomic bomb during the Korean War. Several top military leaders, however, actively suggested and pursued its use because they believed it was proper to utilize any weapon to win. Most notable was Gen. Douglas MacArthur, who, at the start of the war, commanded all United Nations forces in Korea.

As early as July 9, MacArthur had asked the Joint Chiefs of Staff, who controlled the U.S. military, to make atomic bombs available to him. And on December 24, 1950, after the influx of Chinese soldiers pushed UN troops to the brink of defeat,

MacArthur proposed bombing China to make it quit fighting. He later said, "I would have dropped between 30 and 50 atomic bombs [and] spread behind us— from the Sea of Japan to the Yellow Sea— a belt of radioactive cobalt. For at least 60 years there could have been no land invasion of Korea from the north."[121]

But Truman and other U.S. leaders rejected its use. One reason was that although atomic bombs could have destroyed North Korean and Chinese forces, they would also have killed hundreds of thousands, perhaps millions, of civilians. Historian Joseph C. Goulden claims that in addition to their fear of causing such

horrific and needless suffering to so many noncombatants, U.S. officials had another motive not to use the bomb: "Politically, world opinion would not support use of such hellish weapons."[122]

Truman's comments ignited worldwide fears about the bomb because it was Truman who had authorized use of the weapon against Japan; Truman is still the only world leader to have ever committed this weapon to combat. It was a decision Truman said he never regretted because it immediately ended World War II, thus

A panoramic view of the atomic aftermath in Hiroshima shows the devastation caused by a single atomic bomb blast.

saving the lives of hundreds of thousands of soldiers from America and other countries, including Japan, who would have died if fighting had continued.

But in the Korean War, Truman shirked from using the most terrible weapon of mass destruction that had ever been invented. Historian Stanley Sandler believes Truman did this not only because of his fear that it could widen the fighting, possibly into a devastating nuclear war, but for another, far more personal reason: "The U.S. president had no intentions of becoming the only man in history to order twice the dropping of the atomic bomb. For Harry Truman, once was quite enough."[123]

Only a Threat

Although the atomic bomb was not used in Korea, the United States did have bombs available there. In December 1950, after China's entry into the war resulted in a huge setback for UN forces, several nonassembled atomic bombs were quietly transported to a U.S. aircraft carrier off the Korean peninsula. Atomic bombs, however, would remain only a threat the United States could use in trying to negotiate an end to the war.

In 1952 Dwight D. Eisenhower was elected president to succeed Truman, and the general who commanded Allied forces in Europe during World War II did consider the bomb as a weapon of last resort. Eisenhower had campaigned on a promise to end the Korean War, and in early 1953 military leaders again suggested the bomb could win the war.

Eisenhower, however, decided instead to see if he could use fear of the nuclear weapon to intimidate North Korea and China in order to speed up the ongoing peace talks. David Rees, editor of *The Korean War: History and Tactics*, explains:

> Eisenhower was eager to see if threats alone might gain an armistice without having recourse to a major and costly offensive. Accordingly the U.S. ambassador to India leaked the news in February [1953] that the new U.S. Administration was prepared to resort to a nuclear attack upon China, and this was duly [relayed] to the Chinese. Chairman Mao [Tse-tung] had made claims that the atom bomb was a "paper tiger," but he was not a foolish man and probably did not believe his own rhetoric.[124]

Most historians believe the death on February 5, 1952, of Soviet Union leader Joseph Stalin was the key to breaking the deadlock in peace talks; his successor, Georgy M. Malenkov, immediately took a more conciliatory attitude toward ending the conflict. However, the renewed threat of an atomic attack from a president who, as a former military leader, might have been more willing to do whatever it took to win, may also have influenced the Communists to become more serious in negotiating an end to the war.

Also, the Communists by that time might have feared a nuclear attack even earlier in the conflict because the United States in November 1952 had exploded the first hydrogen bomb, a weapon far more powerful than the original atomic bomb. So in the end, the atomic bomb played a part, small though it might have been, in helping to end the Korean War.

Fear Prevented Devastation

Some historians believed that the fact that the United States had such a powerful weapon but refrained from using it in the Korean War was one of the few positive outcomes of that tragic conflict. Military historian S.L.A. Marshall explains that the weapon America did not use had almost as great an impact on the future as the ones it did employ:

> For five years [since the end of World War II] the whole world had been afraid that any small war in which either the United States or Russia [the Soviet Union] took part would quickly turn into an atomic war. Korea was the first test of that dread possibility. The results proved that the atomic powers are fearful of opening "Pandora's Box," and that the possession of arsenals capable of obliterating the world's population has bred in governments a wholly new measure of restraint. This, too, makes the Korean War an important chapter in the story of the twentieth century.[125]

☆ Notes ☆

Introduction: An Unexpected War

1. Quoted in Harold Evans, *The American Century*. New York: Alfred A. Knopf, 1998, p. 423.
2. Quoted in John Toland, *In Mortal Combat: Korea, 1950–1953*. New York: William Morrow, 1991, p. 72.
3. Toland, *In Mortal Combat*, p. 71.
4. Quoted in Max Hastings, *The Korean War*. New York: Simon and Schuster, 1987, p. 255.
5. Joseph C. Goulden, *Korea: The Untold Story of the War*. New York: McGraw-Hill, 1982, p. xvii.
6. George Forty, *At War in Korea*. Shepperton, UK: Ian Allan, 1982, p. 21.

Chapter 1: UN Naval Power Dominates

7. Quoted in Goulden, *Korea*, p. 4.
8. George W. Baer, *One Hundred Years of Sea Power: The U.S. Navy, 1890–1990*. Stanford, CA: Stanford University Press, 1995, p. 344.
9. Stanley Sandler, *The Korean War: No Victors, No Vanquished*. Lexington: University Press of Kentucky, 1999, p. 195.
10. Quoted in Goulden, *Korea*, p. 123.

11. Joseph H. Alexander, *Fleet Operations in a Mobile War: September 1950–June 1951*. Washington, DC: Naval Historical Center, 2001, p. 4.
12. Quoted in Baer, *One Hundred Years of Sea Power*, p. 324.
13. Quoted in Curtis A. Utz, *Assault from the Sea: The Amphibious Landing at Inchon*. Washington, DC: Naval Historical Center, 2000, p. 16.
14. Quoted in Stanley Weintraub, *MacArthur's War: Korea and the Undoing of an American Hero*. New York: Free, 2000, p. 118.
15. Quoted in Utz, *Assault from the Sea*, p. 18.
16. Quoted in Utz, *Assault from the Sea*, p. 27.
17. Quoted in Utz, *Assault from the Sea*, p. 29.
18. Quoted in Alexander, *Fleet Operations in a Mobile War*, p. 25.
19. Baer, *One Hundred Years of Sea Power*, p. 344.
20. Quoted in Alexander, *Fleet Operations in a Mobile War*, p. 41.
21. Quoted in Jon Halliday and Bruce Cumings, *Korea: The Unknown War*. New York: Pantheon Books, 1988, p. 156.

22. Quoted in Rudy Tomedi, ed., *No Bugles, No Drums: An Oral History of the Korean War.* New York: John Wiley & Sons, 1993, p. 154.

Chapter 2: The Korean War: Combat at Close Quarters

23. James Brady, *The Coldest War: A Memoir of Korea.* New York: Thomas Dunne Books, 1990, p. 2.
24. Quoted in U.S. Army, "Close Combat." www.call.army.mil.
25. S.L.A. Marshall, *Infantry Operations and Weapons Usage in Korea: Winter of 1950–51.* Chevy Chase, MD: Johns Hopkins University, 1951, p. 64.
26. Marshall, *Infantry Operations and Weapons Usage in Korea,* p. 99.
27. David Rees, ed., *The Korean War: History and Tactics.* New York: Crescent Books, 1984, p. 89.
28. T.R. Fehrenbach, *This Kind of War: A Study in Unpreparedness.* New York: Macmillan, 1963, p. 669.
29. Forty, *At War in Korea,* p. 15.
30. Quoted in Tomedi, *No Bugles, No Drums,* p. 87.
31. Tomedi, *No Bugles, No Drums,* p. vi.
32. Rees, *The Korean War,* p. 93.
33. Quoted in Tomedi, *No Bugles, No Drums.* 219.
34. Brady, *The Coldest War,* p. 202.
35. Quoted in John M. Glenn, "Cold Steel in Korea," *Military History,* February 2002, p. 54+.
36. Quoted in U.S. Army, "Close Combat."
37. Toland, *In Mortal Combat,* p. 117.

Chapter 3: Tanks, Artillery, and Other Infantry Support Weapons

38. Forty, *At War in Korea,* p. 63.
39. Quoted in Toland, *In Mortal Combat,* p. 81.
40. Forty, *At War in Korea,* p. 63.
41. Quoted in Russel A. Gugeler, *Combat Actions in Korea.* Washington, DC: Office of the Chief of Military History, United States Army, 1970, p. 42.
42. Quoted in David A. Martin, "Ammunition in the Korean War," U.S. Army Logistics Management College. www.almc.army.mil.
43. Quoted in Fehrenbach, *This Kind of War,* p. 668.
44. Quoted in Tomedi, *No Bugles, No Drums,* pp. 224–25.
45. Martin, "Ammunition in the Korean War."
46. Marshall, *Infantry Operations and Weapons Usage in Korea,* p. 93.
47. Marshall, *Infantry Operations and Weapons Usage in Korea,* p. 95.
48. Quoted in Toland, *In Mortal Combat,* p. 83.
49. Quoted in Marshall, *Infantry Operations and Weapons Usage in Korea,* p. 92.
50. Quoted in Tomedi, *No Bugles, No Drums,* p. 101.
51. Quoted in Gugeler, *Combat Actions in Korea,* p. 59.
52. Quoted in John G. Westover, *Combat Support in Korea.* Washington, DC: Center of Military History, United States Army, 1987, p. 230.

53. Carl Bernard, "A Survivor's Guilt," *Newsweek*, March 8, 1999, p. 57.

Chapter 4: Aerial Warfare in the Korean War

54. Robert F. Futrell, *The United States Air Force in Korea, 1950–1953*. Washington, DC: Office of Air Force History, 1983, p. 694.

55. Quoted in Futrell, *The United States Air Force in Korea, 1950–1953*, p. 98.

56. Quoted in Ashley Brown and John Pimlott, eds., *War in Peace: The Marshall Cavendish Illustrated Encyclopedia of Postwar Conflict*, vol. 2. New York: Marshall Cavendish, 1987, p. 370.

57. Quoted in Jim Wilson, *Combat: The Great American Warplanes*. New York: Hearst Books, 2001, p. 49.

58. Quoted in Robert F. Dorr, "Newer MiGs Bedeviled Older B-29s over Korea," *Air Force Times*, July 15, 2002, p. 34.

59. Quoted in Westover, *Combat Support in Korea*, p. 103.

60. Quoted in Walter J. Boyne, "The Forgotten War," *Journal of the Air Force Association Magazine*, June 2000. www.afa.org.

61. Quoted in Jennie Ethell Chancey and William R. Forstchen, eds., *Hotshots: An Oral History of the Air Force Combat Pilots of the Korean War*. New York: William Morrow, 2000, p. 24.

62. Quoted in Rod Paschall, *Witness to War: Korea*. New York: Berkley, 1995, p. 31.

63. Quoted in Tomedi, *No Bugles, No Drums*, p. 26.

64. Quoted in Gugeler, *Combat Actions in Korea*, p. 212.

65. Quoted in Paschall, *Witness to War*, p. 105.

66. Quoted in Tomedi, *No Bugles, No Drums*, p. 163.

67. Quoted in Halliday and Cumings, *Korea*, p. 152.

68. Brady, *The Cold War*, p. 67.

69. Quoted in Westover, *Combat Support in Korea*, p. 113.

70. Quoted in Acepilots.com, "John Glenn: USMC Sabre Jet Pilot, Astronaut." www.acepilots.com.

71. Quoted in Tomedi, *No Bugles, No Drums*, p. 159.

Chapter 5: The Age of Jet Fighter Warfare Begins

72. Quoted in Brown and Pimlott, *War in Peace*, p. 375.

73. Quoted in Wilson, *Combat*, p. 77.

74. Quoted in Sandler, *The Korean War*, p. 171.

75. Quoted in Joe Foss and Matthew Brennan, *Top Guns: America's Fighter Aces Tell Their Stories*. New York: Simon & Schuster, 1991, p. 231.

76. Quoted in U.S. Air Force Military Museum, "Korean War Fiftieth Anniversary." www.wpafb.af.mil.

77. Quoted in Tomedi, *No Bugles, No Drums*, p. 174.

78. Quoted in Tomedi, *No Bugles, No Drums*, p. 174.

79. Quoted in Acepilots.com, "Bud Mahurin on the F-86." www.acepilots.com.

80. Quoted in U.S. Air Force Military Museum, "Korean War Fiftieth Anniversary."

81. Quoted in Tomedi, *No Bugles, No Drums*, p. 174.

82. Hastings, *The Korean War*, p. 261.

83. Chancey and Forstchen, *Hotshots*, p. 163.

84. Chancey and Forstchen, *Hotshots*, p. 163.

85. Quoted in Foss and Brennan, *Top Guns*, p. 292.

86. Quoted in Sheila MacVicar, "Recent Discovery of Russian Presence in Korean War." www.abcnews.go.com.

87. Quoted in MacVicar, "Recent Discovery of Russian Presence in Korean War."

88. Quoted in Acepilots.com, "Bud Mahurin on the F-86."

89. Quoted in Foss and Brennan, *Top Guns*, p. 289.

90. Quoted in Acepilots.com, "John Glenn."

91. Hastings, *The Korean War*, p. 258.

Chapter 6: Psychological Warfare: Words as Weapons

92. Quoted in Weintraub, *MacArthur's War*, p. 32.

93. Quoted in Goulden, *Korea*, p. 86.

94. Quoted in Goulden, *Korea*, p. 86.

95. Quoted in *Encyclopaedia Brittanica CD: 1999 Standard Edition*. Chicago: Encyclopaedia Brittanica, 1999.

96. Stephen E. Pease, *Psywar: Psychological Warfare in Korea, 1950–1953*. Harrisburg, PA: Stackpole Books, 1992, p. xiii.

97. Quoted in Stanley Sandler, *The Korean War: An Encyclopedia*. New York: Garland, 1995, p. 355.

98. Sandler, *The Korean War: An Encyclopedia*, p. 356.

99. Quoted in P.H. Robbs, "Enemy Leaflets of the Korean War," *Falling Leaf*, January 1958. www.btinternet.com.

100. Quoted in Australian War Memorial, "War of Words: Propaganda." www.awm.gov.au.

101. Edgar O'Ballance, *Korea: 1950–1953*. Malabar, FL: Robert E. Krieger, 1985, p. 143.

102. Quoted in Pease, *Psywar*, p. 116.

103. Quoted in James I. Matray, "Revisiting Korea: Exposing Myths of the Forgotten War." www.trumanlibrary.org.

104. Quoted in Sandler, *The Korean War: No Victors, No Vanquished*, p. 247.

105. Quoted in Toland, *In Mortal Combat*, p. 533.

106. Quoted in Toland, *In Mortal Combat*, p. 537.

107. Quoted in John Ellis van Courtland Moon, "The United States and Biological Warfare: Secrets the Early Cold War and Korea," *Bulletin of the Atomic Scientists*, May 1999, p. 70.

108. O'Ballance, *Korea*, p. 141.

109. Quoted in Avalon Project at Yale Law School, "Geneva Convention

(III) Relative to the Treatment of Prisoners of War." www.yale.edu.

110. Quoted in Hastings, *The Korean War*, p. 297.

111. Quoted in Sandler, *The Korean War: No Victors, No Vanquished*, p. 61.

112. Quoted in Toland, *In Mortal Combat*, p. 537.

113. Hastings, *The Korean War*, p. 297.

114. O'Ballance, *Korea*, p. 139.

115. Halliday and Cumings, *Korea*, p. 178.

116. Quoted in Sandler, *The Korean War: An Encyclopedia*, p. 357.

117. Quoted in Pease, *Psywar*, p. xiii.

Conclusion: The Weapon the United States Dared Not Use

118. Quoted in Weintraub, *MacArthur's War*, p. 257.

119. Quoted in Weintraub, *MacArthur's War*, p. 257.

120. Quoted in Samuel Eliot Morison, Henry Steele Commager, and William E. Leuchtenburg, *The Growth of the American Republic*, vol. 2, 6th ed. New York: Oxford University Press, 1969, p. 635.

121. Quoted in Weintraub, *MacArthur's War*, p. 364.

122. Goulden, *Korea*, p. xvi.

123. Sandler, *The Korean War: No Victors, No Vanquished*, p. 191.

124. Rees, *The Korean War*, p. 100.

125. Marshall, *The Military History of the Korean War*, p. 4.

★ For Further Reading ★

Jennie Ethell Chancey and William R. Forstchen, eds., *Hotshots: An Oral History of the Air Force Combat Pilots of the Korean War.* New York: William Morrow, 2000. Pilots explain in their own words what it was like to fight in the Korean War.

Edward F. Dolan, *America in the Korean War.* Brookfield, CT: Millbrook, 1998. An authoritative explanation of the war with many pictures that complement the text.

Joseph C. Goulden, *Korea: The Untold Story of the War.* New York: McGraw-Hill, 1982. In one of the best books written about the war, the author exposes some of the myths that originally surrounded the conflict.

S.L.A. Marshall, *The Military History of the Korean War.* New York: Franklin Watts, 1963. The author, an army officer who served in Korea and later became a top military historian, discusses the war from a strategic point of view.

Rod Paschall, *Witness to War: Korea.* New York: Berkley, 1995. The author uses original source documents and personal narratives to bring the war alive for readers.

John Toland, *In Mortal Combat: Korea, 1950–1953.* New York: William Morrow, 1991. This book by a Pulitzer Prize–winning historian is one of the finest ever written on the Korean War.

Rudy Tomedi, ed., *No Bugles, No Drums: An Oral History of the Korean War.* New York: John Wiley & Sons, 1993. Vivid accounts of the experiences that soldiers had fighting in the Korean War.

✮ Works Consulted ✮

Books

Joseph H. Alexander, *Fleet Operations in a Mobile War: September 1950–June 1951*. Washington, DC: Naval Historical Center, 2001. An overview of how the U.S. Navy fought in the war's first year.

George W. Baer, *One Hundred Years of Sea Power: The U.S. Navy, 1890–1990*. Stanford, CA: Stanford University Press, 1995. The author, who taught maritime strategy at the U.S. Naval War College, has written one of the definitive books on the U.S. Navy.

James Brady, *The Coldest War: A Memoir of Korea*. New York: Thomas Dunne Books, 1990. This best-selling author, who served in Korea as a U.S. Marine lieutenant, paints a vivid picture of what it was like to fight in this war.

Ashley Brown and John Pimlott, eds., *War in Peace: The Marshall Cavendish Illustrated Encyclopedia of Postwar Conflict*. Vol. 2. New York: Marshall Cavendish, 1987. One of a series of books that contains informative essays on topics and issues relating to the military during the decades following World War II.

Encyclopaedia Brittanica CD: 1999 Standard Edition. Chicago: Encyclopedia Brittanica, 1999. One of the best general encyclopedias available.

Harold Evans, *The American Century*. New York: Alfred A. Knopf, 1998. An informative book on U.S. history during the twentieth century.

T.R. Fehrenbach, *This Kind of War: A Study in Unpreparedness*. New York: Macmillan, 1963. The author discusses Korean War weapons and how they were used in battle.

George Forty, *At War in Korea*. Shepperton, UK: Ian Allan, 1982. The author, a British tank officer in Korea, explains what it was like to fight in the war.

Joe Foss and Matthew Brennan, *Top Guns: America's Fighter Aces Tell Their Stories*. New York: Simon and Schuster, 1991. Foss, a World War II Marine Corps ace and Medal of Honor recipient, and his coauthor use personal narratives from pilots to tell the story of aerial combat in the war.

Robert F. Futrell, *The United States Air Force in Korea, 1950–1953*. Washington, DC: Office of Air Force History, 1983. The definitive account of U.S. Air Force activity in the Korean War.

Russell A. Gugeler, *Combat Actions in Korea*. Washington, DC: Office of the Chief of Military History, United States Army, 1970. The author edited official reports by military units that show how soldiers fought and how they reacted during battle to various situations.

Jon Halliday and Bruce Cumings, *Korea: The Unknown War.* New York: Pantheon Books, 1988. These knowledgeable military writers detail how the war was fought, both militarily and politically, while correcting many of the misunderstandings that first existed about the Korean War.

Max Hastings, *The Korean War.* New York: Simon and Schuster, 1987. A solid, sometimes critical look at all aspects of the war.

S.L.A. Marshall, *Infantry Operations and Weapons Usage in Korea: Winter of 1950–51.* Chevy Chase, MD: Johns Hopkins University, 1951. As an officer for the Eighth Army, this future military historian critiques the main weapons U.S. soldiers used in combat.

Samuel Eliot Morison, Henry Steele Commager, and William E. Leuchtenburg, *The Growth of the American Republic.* Vol. 2. 6th ed. New York: Oxford University Press, 1969. An informative retelling of American history by these distinguished historians.

Edgar O'Ballance, *Korea: 1950–1953.* Malabar, FL: Robert E. Krieger, 1985. An insightful look at how both sides fought in the Korean War.

Stephen E. Pease, *Psywar: Psychological Warfare in Korea, 1950–1953.* Harrisburg, PA: Stackpole Books, 1992. One of the most comprehensive books written about this phase of the Korean War.

David Rees, ed., *The Korean War: History and Tactics.* New York: Crescent Books, 1984. The book's chapters, all written by various miltiary experts, discuss different aspects of the Korean War and how it was fought.

Stanley Sandler, *The Korean War: An Encyclopedia.* New York: Garland, 1995. The author explains various subjects related to the war.

———, *The Korean War: No Victors, No Vanquished.* Lexington: University Press of Kentucky, 1999. A vivid, informative, detailed history that includes information on the war that only became available after the downfall of the Soviet Union.

Curtis A. Utz, *Assault from the Sea: The Amphibious Landing at Inchon.* Washington, DC: Naval Historical Center, 2000. An account of the Inchon landing written for the U.S. Navy to help celebrate its fiftieth anniversary.

Stanley Weintraub, *MacArthur's War: Korea and the Undoing of an American Hero.* New York: Free, 2000. The author takes a highly critical look at MacArthur and his role in the Korean War.

John G. Westover, *Combat Support in Korea.* Washington, DC: Center of Military History United States Army, 1987. The author uses personal narratives to explain how engineers and other mostly noncombat soldiers helped support those who did fight in the Korean War.

Jim Wilson, *Combat: The Great American Warplanes*. New York: Hearst Books, 2001. A history of U.S. military aircraft that focuses on some of the best combat planes that ever flew.

Periodicals

Carl Bernard, "A Survivor's Guilt," *Newsweek*, March 8, 1999.

Robert F. Dorr, "Newer MiGs Bedeviled Older B-29s over Korea," *Air Force Times*, July 15, 2002.

John M. Glenn, "Cold Steel in Korea," *Military History*, February 2002.

John Ellis van Courtland Moon, "The United States and Biological Warfare: Secrets from the Early Cold War and Korea," *Bulletin of the Atomic Scientists*, May 1999.

Internet Sources

Acepilots.com, "Bud Mahurin on the F-86." www.acepilots.com.

———, "John Glenn: USMC Sabre Jet Pilot, Astronaut." www.acepilots.com.

Australian War Memorial, "War of Words: Propaganda." www.awm.gov.au.

Avalon Project at Yale Law School. "Geneva Convention (III) Relative to the Treatment of Prisoners of War." www.yale.edu.

Walter J. Boyne, "The Forgotten War," *Journal of the Air Force Association Magazine*, June 2000. www.afa.org.

Hill Goodspeed, "Valor in the Forgotten War." www.history.navy.mil.

Harvey Headland, "Sitting Ducks: Leading the Inchon Invasion." www.usna.com.

Sheila MacVicar, "Recent Discovery of Russian Presence in Korean War." www.abcnews.go.com.

David A. Martin, "Ammunition in the Korean War," U.S. Army Logistics Management College. www.almc.army.mil.

James I. Matray, "Revisiting Korea: Exposing Myths of the Forgotten War." www.trumanlibrary.org.

P.H. Robbs, "Enemy Leaflets of the Korean War," *Falling Leaf*, January 1958. www.btinternet.com.

U.S. Air Force Military Museum, "Korean War Fiftieth Anniversary." www.wpafb.af.mil.

———, "The Story of the MiG-15 on Display." www.wpafb.af.mil.

U.S. Army, "Close Combat." www.call.army.mil.

☆ Index ☆

aerial warfare
  bombers for, 55–57
  cargo aircraft for, 57–58
  dangers in, 64
  destruction of supplies
    and equipment in, 62
  friendly fire and, 60
  helicopters and, 62–63,
    65
  napalm and, 60, 61
  nighttime, 58, 64–65
  as providing support
    for troops in combat,
    58–60
  rocketry, 61
  UN superiority of, 73–75
  see also jet fighters
aircraft carriers, 16–18
airlifts, 58
Alexander, Joseph H., 15,
  25
armed forces
  insufficient American, 14
  reduced after World War
    II, 8
  see also Communist
    forces; pilots; prisoners
    of war; United Nations
    forces
Armentrout, Robert Lee,
  51–52
artillery
  defined, 43
  influencing fortified
    outposts, 43
  types of, 43–44

value of, 43, 45
  see also specific weapons
atomic bomb
  vs. conventional war, 9
  fear of war with, 93–94,
    97
  influencing peace talks,
    96–97
  U.S. mimicking attack by,
    90
  U.S. threat to use, 92,
    94–96
AT-6 Texan, 58
automatic weapons, 29–30

B-26 Invader, 55
B-29 Superfortress, 56–57,
  75
Baer, George W., 12, 23
battleships, 15–16
bayonets, 37–38
bazookas, 48–49
Bedcheck Charlie, 64–65
biological warfare, charges
  of, 86–88
Biteman, Duane E., 56, 60
Black Tuesday, 57
Bloody Ridge, 60
bombers, 55–57
Bordelon, Guy, 65
Brady, James, 26, 63
Brady, Joseph, 35, 36
Brennan, Matthew, 61
Brentlinger, Jay, 64
British weapons, 28
Brooks, Charles, 35

Brown, Russell J., 67, 69
Browning automatic rifle
  (BAR), 29–30

C-47 Skytrain, 57
C-54 Skymaster, 57
C-119 Flying Boxcar, 57
Capps, Arlie G., 18
carbine, 29
cargo aircraft, 57–58
Carpenter, Vail P., 25
Carter, Doug, 71, 72
casualties
  aerial warfare, 64
  at Inchon landing, 21
Chambers, Loran, 40
Chancey, Jennie Ethell,
  74–75
China
  battle tactics, 33, 34
  charges of biological
    warfare by, 87
  weapons used by, 30–31
  see also Communist
    forces
Chou En-lai, 87
Clausewitz, Carl von,
  26–27
Collins, Tom, 73
Communist forces
  basic infantry weapons
    used by, 30–33
  battle tactics, 33–34
  fighter jets of, 70–71
  mortars used by, 47–48
  piloting skills of, 74–75

propaganda by, 92–93,
   84, 86–88
repatriation of prisoners
   of war by, 91–92
sea mines and, 22–23, 25
treatment of prisoners of
   war by, 88–90
UN naval superiority
   over, 24–25
see also China; North
   Korea; Soviet Union
Condron, Andrew, 88
Corsairs, 17
Cumings, Bruce, 90

Eighth Army, 14
Einstein, Albert, 94
Ennis, Bob, 62
Essex (aircraft carrier),
   15

F-51 Mustang, 55, 56
F-80 Shooting Star, 55,
   67–69
F-82 Mustang, 54, 55
F-84 Thunderjet, 55
F-86 Sabre, 55
   in combat, 77–78
   as fun to fly, 69
   improvement in, 69–70
   limitations of, 76–77
   vs. MiG 15, 71–72
   scarcity of, 68, 75–76
   shooting down a MiG, 71
Fehrenbach, T.R., 32, 44
Fernandez, Manuel J., 66
Fifth Cavalry, 37–38
fighter planes. *See* jet
   fighters
First Marine Division, 19
Fischer, Harold, 61, 74
flamethrowers, 52
Flying Fish Channel, 18

Forstchen, William R.,
   74–75
Forty, George, 11, 33, 39,
   41
Foss, Joe, 61
Fraser, Carl, 54
friendly fire, 60
Futrell, Robert F., 53, 58

Geneva Convention, 88
Gerard, Robert J., 36
Glenn, John, 64, 77–78
Göring, Hermann, 55
Gorshkov, Sergei G., 15
Goulden, Joseph C., 9, 95
grenades, 30, 32, 38
guns. *See specific weapons*

Halliday, Jon, 90
Hammond, William C., Jr.,
   52
hand grenades, 30, 32, 38
Harrison, William K., 86
Hastings, Max, 73, 78, 90
Headland, Harvey, 22
helicopters, 62–63, 65
Hill 180, 37
Hinton, Bruce H., 73
Hiroshima attack, 9, 57
HMS *Triumph* (British
   aircraft carrier), 15
howitzers, 44
Hudson, William G., 54
Hungnam evacuation, 23
hydroelectric generating
   plants, 62

Inchon landing
   casualties, 21
   landing ship tank as vital
      to, 20
   planning of, 18–19
   ships for, 19

Sitting Ducks and, 22
   timing of, 20–21
Iowa (battleship), 15

Jabara, James, 66
jet fighters, 54–55
   in combat, 74, 77–78
   F-86 vs. MiGs, 71–72
   first Korean War battle
      with, 67–68
   historical development
      of, 67
   pilots of, 66–67
   UN and, 68–70
   limitations of, 75–77
   see also aerial warfare
Joint Task Force Seven, 19
Joswiak, Cass J., 58
Joy, Turner, 92

Ki, Wun Hong, 60
Koelsch, John Kelvin, 65
Korea
   devastation of, 62
   geography of, 12
   see also North Korea;
      South Korea

landing ship tank (LST),
   19, 20
land mines, 47
Lawson, Fred, 33
leaflet propaganda, 81–83
Lexington (aircraft carrier),
   15
Lilley, Bill, 75
long-range guns, 44–47
"Long Tom," 44

M-1 rifles
   improvements in, 26
   physical description of,
      27, 29

as a sniper rifle, 29
MacArthur, Douglas
  on the atomic bomb,
    94–95
  on devastation of Korea,
    62
  Inchon landing plan by,
    18–19
machine guns, 51–52
Mahurin, Walker "Bud,"
  69, 72, 76–77
main line of resistance, 3
  5
Malenkov, Georgy M., 96
Mao Tse-tung, 86
Marshall, S.L.A., 29, 48, 97
Martin, David A., 45, 46
McConnell, Joseph, 66–67
McGill, E.J., 57
MiG Alley, 76
MiG 15, 55
  B-29s and, 57
  cannons of, 70–71
  F-80s attacked by, 67–68
  vs. F-86 Sabre, 71–72
  F-86 shooting down, 71
  number of, 75
  physical description of,
    70
  U.S. receiving, 73
"Mighty Mo, the." See
  Missouri
military equipment. See
  weapons; specific weapons
Millett, Lewis L., 37
mines
  land, 47
  sea, 22–23, 25
Missouri (battleship),
  15–16
Moon Tip Island, 18, 20,
  22
mortars, 43, 44, 47–48

mosquito missions, 58
Murray, R.L., 49
Myers, Frank Baldwin, 38

Nagasaki attack, 9, 57
napalm bombs, 60, 61
National Security Council,
  87
navy. See United Nations
  forces, naval
Neal, George M., 65
negotiations
  atomic bomb
    influencing, 96–97
  first efforts of, 35
  propaganda and, 86
New Jersey (battleship), 15
nighttime warfare
  aerial, 58, 64–65
  by Chinese troops, 33
No, Kum-Sok, 72, 73
North Korea
  attack on South Korea, 7
  defection of pilot from,
    73
  naval strength, 12
  nighttime aerial warfare
    and, 64–65
  political justification for
    attack by, 79
  Soviets supplying arms
    to, 10–11
  Soviet tanks used by,
    39–41
  superiority of weapons
    of, 11
  see also Communist
    forces
North Korean People's
  Army. See Communist
  forces
nuclear war. See atomic
  bomb

O'Ballance, Edgar, 85,
  90–91
Operation Chromite. See
  Inchon landing
ordnance, 53

Pace, Frank, Jr., 92
Panthers, 17
Parker, Jerry, 78
Paschall, Rod, 36
peace talks. See
  negotiations
Pease, Stephen E., 80, 92
pilots
  Communist forces,
    74–75
  cooperation among
    American, 77–78
  defection of North
    Korean, 73
  helicopter, 65
  as heroes, 66–67
  Soviet, 75
  superiority of American,
    73–74
Pirate (minesweeper),
  22
pistols, 29
planes. See aerial warfare;
  jet fighters
Pledge (minesweeper),
  22
Porter, Ira, 71
Princeton (aircraft
  carrier), 15
prisoners of war (POWs)
  brainwashing, 90–91
  reeducation of American,
    81
  repatriation of
    Communist, 91–92
  torture of, 88
  treatment of UN, 88–90

propaganda
  charges of biological
    warfare and, 86–88
  defined, 80
  by Harry S. Truman,
    79–80
  by Kim Il Sung, 79
  with leaflets, 81–83, 84
  with loudspeakers, 83,
    85
  with radio, 83
  U.S. vs. Soviets winning
    global support with,
    85–86
psychological warfare. See
  prisoners of war,
  propaganda
Pusan Perimeter, 18, 60

recoilless rifles, 50–51
Red Baron, the. See
  Richthofen, Manfred von
Rees, David, 28, 30, 35, 43,
  96
Republic of Korea. See
  South Korea
Richthofen, Manfred von,
  67
Rickenbacker, Eddie, 67
Ridgway, Matthew B., 43,
  81
Robinson, Anthony, 54
rockets, 61
Roy, Robert, 40

Samoilov, Dmitri, 75
sampans, 25
Sandler, Stanley, 12–13,
  82, 89, 96
sea mines, 22–23, 25
semiautomatic weapons,
  27, 29
Seoul (South Korea), 21

Service, Jim, 17, 64
Seventh Army Infantry
  Division, 19
Sherman tank, 41
ships
  for Inchon landing, 19
  UN aircraft carriers,
    16–17
  UN battleships, 15–16
  U.S. Navy, 17–18
Shpagin Pistolet-
  PulemyotShpagina (PPSh
  41) submachine gun, 32
Sitting Ducks of Inchon,
  22
Skyraiders, 17
Smith, Allan E., 22–23
Smith, Charles B., 14, 40
sniper rifle, 29
soldiers
  helicopters and
    wounded, 63
  on M-1 rifles, 29
  see also pilots; prisoners
    of war
sortie, 53
South Korea
  aircraft of, 53–54
  North Korean attack of, 7
  see also United Nations
    forces
Soviet Union
  arms supplied by, 10–11
  atomic bomb and, 93–94,
    96–97
  pilots of, 75
  propaganda by, 85–86
  tanks of, 39–41
  see also Communist
    forces
Stalin, Joseph, 85–86
Stratemeyer, George E., 58
Struble, Arthur D., 19

submachine guns, 31–32
Swenson, David H., 22

T-34 tank, 39–41
tanks, Soviet, 39–41
Task Force Smith, 14,
  39–41
38th parallel, 34–35
"thought reform," 90–91
Tokarev semiautomatic
  (TT33), 32
Toland, John, 9, 38
Tomedi, Rudy, 35
Tosques, Nick, 46, 81
Truman, Harry S., 54
  on the atomic bomb,
    95–96
  propaganda by, 79–80, 85
Tuz, Curtis A., 20

United Nations forces
  air attacks supporting
    ground troops by, 59–60
  air superiority of, 53–54
  artillery used by, 43–44
  attacked by Soviet tanks,
    40–41
  basic infantry weapons
    used by, 27–30
  battle tactics, 34
  jet fighters of, 68–70
  lack of weapons by, 52
  leaflet propaganda by,
    81–82
  mortars used by, 47
  naval
    blockading of ports by,
      23–24
    fleet of, 15–18
    Inchon landing and,
      18–21
    mines at Wonsan island
      and, 22–23

vs. North Korean naval strength, 12–13
superiority over Communist forces, 24–25
U.S. Navy's help in strengthening, 14–15
tanks used by, 41–42
treatment of prisoners of war by, 88–90
U.S. manpower and war material for, 10
value of artillery for, 46–47
United States
aerial superiority of, 54
charges of biological warfare against, 87–88
mimicking of atomic bomb attack by, 90
propaganda by, 79–80, 85
threat to use the atomic bomb by, 93, 94–96
treatment of POWs from, 88–90
as unprepared for Korean War, 7–9, 13–14
U.S. Air Force, 90

U.S. Navy
Hungnam evacuation by, 23–24
men and supplies transported to Korea by, 15
vessels, 17–18
see also United Nations forces, naval

Valley Forge (aircraft carrier), 15, 16–17
Vandenberg, Hoyt S., 62
vehicles, 42
Voice of America, 83
Voice of the UN Command, 83

Walker, Walton H., 60
Walsh, Vincent, 25
weapons
basic Communist, 30–33
basic UN, 27–30
mortars, 47–48
as not differing from WWII weapons, 9–10
placed in Europe vs. Asia, 8

poor shape of American, 8–9
silencing of, 36
Soviet Union supplying, 10–11
tactics influenced by, 33–34
UN lack of, 52
used at close quarters, 26–27
see also aerial warfare; artillery; atomic bomb; specific weapons
Wilkins, James V., 65
Wilson, Jim, 67
Winter, Arnold, 60
Wisconsin (battleship), 15
Wolmi-do. See Moon Tip Island
Wonsan island, 22–23, 24

Yeager, Chuck, 73
Yorktown (aircraft carrier), 15
Young, Richard O., 25

Zonge, George, 50–51

★ Picture Credits ★

Cover Photo: © Hulton/Archive
Associated Press, AP, 38, 45
© Bettmann/CORBIS, 46, 49, 63
© Horace Bristol/CORBIS, 68
© CORBIS, 10, 24, 50, 54, 56, 61
© Corel Corporation, 42
© George Hall/CORBIS, 74
© Hulton/Archive, 8, 16, 27, 28, 51, 59 (both), 76, 77, 82, 84 (both), 86, 87, 94
National Archives, 19, 21, 31 (top), 32, 36, 89, 91
Brandy Noon, 13
© Reuters NewMedia Inc./CORBIS, 70
© Smithsonian Institution, 95
U.S. Army/Courtesy Harry S. Truman Library, 80
West Point Museum, 31 (bottom)

★ About the Author ★

Michael V. Uschan has written nearly thirty books, including *The Korean War,* for which he won the 2002 Council of Wisconsin Writers Juvenile Nonfiction Award. Mr. Uschan began his career as a writer and editor with United Press International, a wire service that provided stories to newspapers, radio, and television. Journalism is sometimes called "history in a hurry." Mr. Uschan considers writing history books a natural extension of the skills he developed in his many years as a working journalist. He and his wife, Barbara, reside in the Milwaukee suburb of Franklin, Wisconsin.